ROUTLEDGE LIBRARY EDITIONS: AGING

Volume 1

FACING RETIREMENT

FACING RETIREMENT

A Guide for the Middle Aged and Elderly

A COUNTRY DOCTOR

R Routledge
Taylor & Francis Group

LONDON AND NEW YORK

First published in 1960 by George Allen & Unwin Ltd, Second Edition 1964

This edition first published in 2024
by Routledge
4 Park Square, Milton Park, Abingdon, Oxon OX14 4RN

and by Routledge
605 Third Avenue, New York, NY 10158

Routledge is an imprint of the Taylor & Francis Group, an informa business

British Library Cataloguing in Publication Data
A catalogue record for this book is available from the British Library

ISBN: 978-1-032-67433-9 (Set)
ISBN: 978-1-032-69422-1 (Volume 1) (hbk)
ISBN: 978-1-032-69435-1 (Volume 1) (pbk)
ISBN: 978-1-032-69434-4 (Volume 1) (ebk)

DOI: 10.4324/9781032694344

Publisher's Note
The publisher has gone to great lengths to ensure the quality of this reprint but points out that some imperfections in the original copies may be apparent.

Disclaimer
The publisher has made every effort to trace copyright holders and would welcome correspondence from those they have been unable to trace.

FACING RETIREMENT

*A Guide for the Middle Aged
and Elderly*

by

A Country Doctor

M.A., M.D.
President Oxfordshire Association
for the Care of Old People

WITH A FOREWORD BY
THE LATE
J. W. ROBERTSON SCOTT
C.H., M.A. (HON.) OXON

Ruskin House
GEORGE ALLEN & UNWIN LTD
MUSEUM STREET LONDON

FIRST PUBLISHED IN 1960

SECOND IMPRESSION 1961

SECOND EDITION 1964

PRINTED IN GREAT BRITAIN
in 11 pt. *Pilgrim type*
BY EAST MIDLAND PRINTING CO. LTD.
BURY ST. EDMUNDS, SUFFOLK

TO MY WIFE

CONTENTS

FOREWORD

by

J. W. Robertson Scott c.h., m.a. (Hon) Oxon.

F o r half my thirty-eight years in the Cotswolds I have had my eye on my friend and neighbour the Author. He interested me because of the life he was leading.

The demands of a busy profession did not keep him from following me as representative of the locality on the Rural District Council and then on the County Council. Before and after that in speechmaking, at conferences, in letters to the Press, and ultimately in the Chairmanship of the County Association for the Care of Old People, he devoted himself to the physical, mental and social problems of old age as brought closely under his observation in his villages. First hand knowledge—he once made a notable survey of the problems of living alone—and his conspicuous common sense obviously played their part. There has been no end to his local activities. I recall not only opening, for the Rural District Council, bungalows of a new type for the elderly in the planning of which he had a share, but planting a tree on a piece of public ground he had had levelled and grassed.

I write this Foreword because, besides knowing him well, I know a thing or two about books. Have I not written 29, and in the course of a life continuing into the nineties incurred the responsibility of reviewing something like a couple of thousand? I cite this experience because it may carry some weight when I say that the present volume is out of the ordinary, and that it handles practically and with pains, knowledge, and consideration, the problems of becoming elderly, which we must all become in turn. Here is not only information new to most people but information which they will be glad to have. The book is human on domestic relations, always plain spoken, surprisingly wide in range, simply expressed, easily read, and kind.

9

It is not so much about the elderly as for them, and should make an ideal gift for anyone in the fifties or sixties. I am pleased to have a small share in getting the volume known.

PREFACE

T H I S book is the result of the experience of a singlehanded village doctor who has had the day-to-day care of virtually a whole community rich and poor for nearly twenty-five years. It was written to try to fill a need known to be felt by many. It was conceived during a course of lectures delivered five years ago at Denman College, the country headquarters of the Women's Institute movement in Berkshire: another class last autumn gave approval to the substance.

Most readers, especially the more elderly, will be wise to ignore the order in which the chapters are presented and to dip here and there as fancy and interest please. The scope of the book is wide, but wider still are the distances between the outlook of those about to retire, those in the later years of retirement, and those who have the care of the old and the aged. The view of any individual reader is likely to be relatively narrow, and it may be difficult for some to accept what is outside or at variance with their personal experience. For example those who have been happily married for forty or fifty years may not readily understand the problems of people who live alone or are lonely, and will probably resent the mere thought of living with others however unlikely it may be; yet they should find much that is acceptable in other chapters which deal with matters which touch them more closely.

No matter how many your years may be, if you can pick up a point here and there it is proof that you are not aged but at most merely old; there should be more profit for those who are approaching retirement or are in its earlier years. It is hoped it will prove a helpful guide to them on their journey into the interesting but unmapped country which lies ahead. It may also enable many a little better to understand older relatives and friends, together with their doubts and anxieties.

No one has the whole truth on any matter, and indeed what is truth varies with time and circumstances. We learn much and often modify our opinions if we listen to those whose viewpoints differ from our own, thus coming a step or two nearer wisdom. The author will be pleased and helped to hear from any readers who care to give him the benefit of their experience and will write to him through the publishers.

JUNE 1960

Preface to the Second Edition

This new edition recognises that preparation for retirement, as much as retirement itself, now interests an increasing number of people. It also studies the part a woman can play, the changing face of marriage, and the potential happiness (and difficulties) of companionship in the later years, whilst fresh attention has been given to money matters.

But the body of the original book remains almost unchanged and these new thoughts are additions which it is hoped will be as welcome as the old.

JUNE 1964

ACKNOWLEDGEMENTS

E X T R A C T S from certain chapters appeared as articles in the *Belfast News Letter, Bolton Evening News, Glasgow Evening Times, Mansfield Chronicle, Oxford Times, Portsmouth Evening News, Rochdale Observer, Rugby Advertiser, West Briton,* and *Yorkshire Evening Post* in 1958, and attracted many letters which had a considerable influence on their final form. I am obliged to the Editors of these papers and their readers for their interest.

In his contributed chapter Mr Robertson Scott acknowledges his indebtedness to the Editor of *The Listener* for permission to reprint some extracts from his broadcast talk published therein, and to his thanks I add my own.

Too many friends and colleagues helped me with advice and guidance in the preparation of this book for it to be possible for me to name them all, deeply grateful to them though I am. The foundations were laid by Mrs C. R. S. Williams, who did the field work in 1954 of our survey into the needs of old people living alone, and by Mr C. H. Hudson, Editor of the *Oxford Times*, who gave space for its publication and has always encouraged and helped. Mr A. H. Flemming, octogenarian of Oxford and friendly critic who is not above quoting scripture to his purpose, and Miss E. G. Preddy D.N. of Oxford, have done much to bring the volume into its present form.

Miss Mary Walton has given me clerical assistance at once without price and beyond price: her 'always ready' willingness to devote her spare time to the drudgery of retyping and typing again, and her quiet encouragement when there was difficulty or disappointment, were major factors in bringing our labours to completion.

My wife and family have provided a peaceful background and affectionate understanding, to which has been added the goodwill of many patients. These have been an immeasurable comfort to a sometimes harassed medical practitioner, which I acknowledge with gratitude.

THE AUTHOR

GLOSSARY

For the purpose of this book

PENSIONABLE AGE is taken as approximately 65 in men, 60 in women.

RETIREMENT is taken to commence at about 65. Policemen retire at 45, bank managers at 60: on the other hand some people are still doing a good day's work at 80.

THE LATER YEARS is that part of retirement, usual after 75, when activity is considerably reduced. (It could be called 'Old age' but for many it is a pleasanter period of life than is implied to most by these words).

THE MIDDLE-AGED are those who are in the fifties and early sixties and graduate to become

THE ELDERLY the senior citizens, mostly active, a few years either side of 65, who in turn become

OLD PEOPLE when they have advanced into the later years but have no great physical disabilities, or little regard for any which they may have.

THE AGED are those who are feeble whatever their total of years.

OLD AGE is mentioned in passages here and there as an alternative to 'the later years'.

Chapter 1

THE OTHER SIDE OF THE HILL

A wise physician instructs the healthy
Emperor Huang-Ti of China 2,700 B.C.

SIR WALTER SCOTT used to call later life 'reaching the other side of the hill'—retirement was hardly thought of in his day a hundred and more years ago. It is a pleasanter phrase than 'the downhill of life'. Yet both give promise of an easier road now the summit has been passed. Though the wind will not be as good and the limbs will tire more readily, the helpful slope conceals these drawbacks and if there is a favourable breeze from behind it can be a very pleasant phase indeed.

For the many who keep their health, strain and struggle are much less than on the uphill road and then, too, the view was blocked by the slope ahead. Now there is time for thought, and though the horizon is mist and shadow, there is a wide prospect.

We need to place our feet more carefully than when climbing, and to watch for obstacles of which we have no experience but which are there none the less. A fall on a downhill slope must aye be more heavy than a slip on an upward one; it is harder to recover from it, and the knowledge thus acquired of one kind of difficulty may not help us to avoid another.

A pension on reaching the age of retirement is now the right of everyone. The day when it is first received is a milestone which most people pass with a peculiar sense of achievement. For some the satisfaction is lessened by compulsory departure from the habits of a lifetime; for others there is the opportunity of continuing the customary work to a lessening extent or of branching out into a new sphere of activity. But it is well to take advantage of the reminder that the years are slipping away. In this country more than one thousand people reach pensionable age every day, and it is estimated that at present they total more than six million. By 1980 when those now in the early fifties will be retired, they are expected to number between nine and ten million.

Though to reach the age of retirement is an achievement, it is sad that so many face unnecessary difficulties when they do so —but sadder still if they encounter and are defeated by them later. The steady increase in the number of pensioners and their claims on society, and the progressively decreasing proportion of those who have to carry the burden, make it a matter of national importance that the weight on the younger generations shall be lightened in every possible way.

People usually begin to notice disabilities due to increasing years when they are about 50, and to feel their age around 70; but we vary so much. Sooner or later will come a day when we begin to realize that old age is affecting us as well as other people, and suddenly feel a wave of intimate sympathy with the frail for whom previously we had but pity. In and after middle age it is necessary to accustom oneself to lessening powers, and to be mindful of the change when finding difficult something hitherto done with little effort. It need be no more than that, for there will be compensations, not least of which is the escape from the routine imposed by having to earn a living; and the resulting sense of freedom can be quite delicious to those who have prepared themselves for it.

Mature men and women are not afraid of advancing years. True, most rather resent any realization that they are growing older, and tend to look away or to turn their backs. Yet if there is reasonable health and independence and freedom from major anxieties, retirement can be as interesting a phase of life as any of the earlier ones; in some ways it may be more pleasant, in others it will be less so, but it still has its share of changes even though the power of adaptation to them lessens. As the years slip by, most find it increasingly difficult to improvise as they have done in the past, to maintain skills which call for speed of action or to learn new ones, and to find new interests though their minds continue to keep fully active. Exercise of any kind more readily tires, physical powers are limited within narrowing bounds, minor disabilities may force themselves on the notice and linger there. But it is also true, even if there seem to

be no fresh horizons and the circle of interests and acquaintances is contracting, that more value is attached to family
relationships and the understanding companionship of friends.
Most find the hours pass too quickly for the days to be filled as
fully as they would like.

Nowadays people expect to reach pensionable age, and
would be disappointed if they felt that they might not. Until a
few years ago it was looked upon only as a possibility, and for
the majority neither a very attractive nor a very welcome one.
The greatest need of middle-aged people is forethought so that
retirement may be as healthy and secure and contented as
possible. This calls for willingness to listen and think and learn.
There must be some preparation both for the earlier and the
later stages of retirement if they are to be happy, and the time
to prepare is when they are being approached.

It is a matter of experience that around retiring age guidance
is not only acceptable to most but by many is actively desired.
Wise women never retire, though they often grow old. It is a
curious fact that in general they suffer more from ill-health
than men of equal age, yet live longer on the average by about
five years. This is partly because they keep working in spite of
their infirmities, and partly because they continue in the groove
established early in adult life. Men are less fortunate: a major
change in occupation and interests is sooner or later thrust on
them as it is on business and professional women.

'In fact old age is not necessarily a cause of unhappiness. The
discontents of later life have their roots in character more than
in events.' So the Greek philosopher Plato wrote over 2,500
years ago, and his observation is as true today as it was then. It
is convenient to forget the difficulties of childhood, and the
physical pains by which over the years of growth we learned
from experience. It is convenient to forget the strains and
frustrations of growing-up, adolescence, though these exist for
many and some find them an intolerable burden. It is convenient
to forget the anxieties of the different phases of adult life,
because when people look back they mostly like to count only
the sunny hours, like a sundial; yet almost nothing can happen
to those over 70 which can cause the distress of mind or body

which somehow they managed to live through in the past. All ages have their problems, but in retirement a solution can be found to most save those which are or which become beyond physical powers: it is necessary to learn to accept the last as gracefully as possible.

People in the later years live a slower tempo, counting themselves mellowed like good wine and to be treated as gently. If they are leisurely in going upstairs, they should not be thought to be at death's door. When they face an escalator they are usually not too proud to say thank you to one who helps. They enjoy their lives by being happy, and useful to others, without going at an express rate.

Medical science is doing much to make it possible to exceed the three score years and ten of the psalmist, and to go on to his four score years of 'labour and sorrow' with more health and well-being and happiness than could have been expected even as recently as twenty years ago! Because disease is being checked and controlled, and because so much more is being done through the social services, increasing numbers are living through the seventies and well into the eighties and even into the nineties. But no one has yet found a way to prevent bodies from wearing out.

An old friend remarked to me that the happiest years of his life were those between 70 and 80, and as he was then over 90 he was in a position fairly to judge. Even when the latest years creep up they are a period of content to many, and should be to many more; most will by then have reached a stage when they will not take kindly to change and (very reasonably) will do everything they can to avoid it. Moreover the world will be different from the one they formerly knew, and the people; they have but little part in it, and so they retire more and more into themselves. This is why it is so important that people should prepare themselves and their ways. In old age all are at a disadvantage in trying to deal with any difficulty which may arise because minds and bodies are inevitably and naturally less flexible.

Chapter 2

PLANNING RETIREMENT

All the keys hang not at one man's girdle
English Proverb sixteenth century

I

A N elderly couple inherited a cottage with a pleasant view at the top of a hill, about a mile out of a village; it had a large garden, and they felt they had everything they wanted because although they were strangers to the district they had plenty to occupy them. For a while, indeed, they were content. But as the years crept by the hill seemed to become steeper and longer: shopping became a problem, because of the distance from the village: the weather increasingly kept them indoors: when there was illness there were no near neighbours and little help paid or unpaid to hand: finally the garden which had been their pride and joy became an effort, then it became a labour and anxiety, and gradually they had to let more and more of it remain untended. They had put over-much of their capital into the house, improving it without thought whether one day they might not need their money for more necessary things, and the rapid disappearance of what had appeared adequate savings caused them anxiety.

Such stories are innumerable, and the sad part is the utter helplessness of those who have looked forward to a happy retirement, but have not planned wisely for those later years which they hope and expect to attain. It is not suggested that too much thought should be given to the distant future: September or October is too soon to be thinking about Christmas. But with a little consideration what is desired and what is wise usually can fairly be matched, and it is important that they should. People differ widely in likes and dislikes, abilities, interests and so on: when looking to the future, if they plan at all each will tend to plan differently from his fellows, and the problems they will encounter will vary as greatly as their personalities and circumstances. By the time they have reached the age of retirement most have learned to look ahead; what many lack is understanding of the probable course of events thereafter.

II

The principal problems of retirement have been found to arise from lack of occupation, loss of income, decreased strength, defects of health, and impairment of hearing or sight or the sense of balance. Few will escape one or other of these in the long run, so it is practical to think about them when looking positively towards it.

If there is agreement between husband and wife on their plans for retirement, the views of adult children (by now themselves people with responsibilities) are not of the first importance, but they should be obtained because sensible suggestions may be made. There can also be a fuller feeling of family responsibility, which may be helpful to the parents in later years. It is surprising how many men do not consult even their wives about what they intend to do, much less their children. Yet so much happiness in retirement is found in partnership.

There are some who urge that retirement should mark the commencement of a new adventure in living. In a sense it is, but in truth the time for adventure and experimenting is beforehand, when thought is being given to plans which it will not be easy to alter in old age. Too often retirement is treated like a new chapter in a book; one day a man is employed, as he has been for years; the next he is not, but says vaguely that he looks forward to doing all the things for which he had often wished in the past that he had the time. This sort of thing works out badly for most. No one really likes suddenly to feel that his life's work has been left behind him and that he seems to be through; for life without purpose—as it must then seem to so many—is life without meaning.

A man of mature mind will consider the prospect of retirement when he is in his fifties, and try so to widen his interests that it will be to, as well as from, something. It is not always possible for it to be gradual, though desirable that it should be, and it is usually sensible to have some occupation after the end of 'work'. The lucky ones can make the years after 60 the stepping-down age, and continue in familiar but lessening duties for a varying time during which other interests can be cultivated. Those who are under compulsion to change their lives completely at 65 are less fortunate. Worst off, of course, are the 20 per cent who are compelled to it by ill-health, but even for them life may yet hold a great deal of happiness. It is true that there are those who after a lifetime of heavy or tedious work have a great and natural desire to rest, and providing they can find some other quiet interest in life this may be wise for them. But for most, moderate activity is more likely to be helpful providing they live within the limits of their capacities and avoid overstrain of mind or body.

Many people in the active years of early retirement would be better off if they set out to earn a little. The money will for most be less important than the interest it can bring. Indeed, if everybody coming up to retirement would put themselves in the way of earning a little later on, not only would they be helping the community but there would be less moaning about the retirement pension. It is for elderly people to care for, help and be friendly with the old and aged and if possible they should be paid for it. Many old people have disabilities, and the aged can not work, for no one is really aged who can, but most elderly people are only getting their second wind: none can understand the aged so well.

There are a hundred and one little jobs for men and women to do if they choose to look for them, from baby sitting or raising seedlings to helping in a small shop for an hour or two a day, or in some way using the special skills they possess like book-keeping or teaching or repairing china. What is not advisable is doing anything which needs capital beyond a few pounds or whatever can easily be spared; it might get lost, however promising the prospects may seem to be, and there will be no opportunity to earn more. It is not easy, and is usually unwise, late in life to start enterprises which are new. Before retirement is the time to find out by trial and error what is liked and what suits, not trusting to later half-thought-out inclinations.

Hobbies in themselves are rarely a satisfactory solution of the problem of 'time to spare' unless they are constructive; in any event there should be more than one. People want to be doing something useful and not just filling in the days. Far greater satisfaction is derived from creative occupations like gardening —but two men in one garden are usually as upsetting to the peace as two women in one kitchen—carpentry, public work or even keeping chickens, than from the purely diversional ones such as collecting stamps or reading: though a mixture of both is best. The wireless and long playing records are completely altering retirement for many; to no others, not even children, is television so valuable, although the old may find it tiring.

III

People need their own private corner surrounded by their personal possessions which have associations, and women at least will rarely find this in the home of another. When in our own we need never be bored: there is always something to do. Most will continue to live where they are already, usually because they have little option; but if they have a choice it should be a matter of careful thought. So many have the wrong kind of house in the wrong place, and forethought now may save unendurable hardship another day. A home suitable for a family will usually be too large and inconvenient for one or two elderly or old people in these times when help is scarce and dear. It may be necessary to choose between the associations of many years, and the likelihood of future inconvenience or difficulty. If change there is to be, then the sooner the better after the children leave home and parents are on their own.

In general a well-situated small house, ground floor flat, or bungalow, with labour saving conveniences, is the ideal. It is difficult for people in their sixties to realise how limited is the accommodation old age needs. Stairs usually cause much difficulty to the old, even when health is good. Most will find it unwise to live altogether upstairs because heavy things like coal, ashes and shopping will have to be carried up or down; and some of the bodily disabilities of old age which may afflict us, like physical weakness, a tired heart, arthritis, or impaired vision or giddiness, may be made almost intolerable by stair-climbing where otherwise they could be quite bearable.

If it is decided to change house, it is usually undesirable to go to a strange place, except for people who are good mixers and not too old to mix. It is best to keep roots in familiar soil, and to be near to family and friends; even for those who like the country or seaside it could be a mistake to move there. It is unwise to be outside a village or on the fringe of a town: one day there may be handicaps, so to get a new home which is away from buses and shops is a mistake. As a general rule it is also a mistake to choose to live in a busy street where traffic will make crossing the road dangerous. Nearness to centres like the church or chapel, cinema, bowls or old people's club or public house or other interests, as well as the necessary shops, will make a big difference later. Half a mile which we can now walk in ten or twelve minutes will then seem a very long way indeed with parcels to carry, even in good weather; and what is now quite a slight slope will seem to be a hill in ten years time. There are so many disappointments and so much unhappiness which could easily be prevented.

Nor should we forget to give thought to our neighbours. Good ones are a godsend in a time of difficulty, one bad one is always a drawback. We have to be willing to be good neighbours ourselves. It is remarkable how small groups of elderly people can get together to help each other out—when they get to know each other well enough, sometimes even going so far as to prepare a communal meal once or twice a week to save the burden of cooking, or for two to take turn and turn about.

When we are old we will not want to move house again. The wiser of two choices may not be the more attractive at present, but may save much discomfort in the future.

IV

When buying a house, if you buy trouble you will pay for it at least twice. Before you start to look round for one to purchase, consult a good solicitor—not necessarily the nearest one—and when you have found your house don't sign anything until he tells you to. If there is no purchase his advice will cost you very little: if the deal goes through he will make no charge extra to his usual fees. You will probably need to have him draw up the final contract: he may as well be in at the beginning.

You are likely to buy your house through an agent. He is employed by the owner. He only gets paid if he sells the house. At best he won't tell you a deliberate untruth, and will give you a straight answer to a straight question, though it won't be in writing. But he may be nothing more than a sharp salesman. He is not your friend, but his employer's. He may be persuasive and charming: but the more he seems to be on your side, the more unethical he is—and the more you need a good solicitor at your side to take the pen out of your hand before you unsuspectingly sign an irrevocable contract.

The seller is bound only by the terms of the written contract, no matter what he or his agent may tell you or promise. Dreams and nightmares have this in common: they happen when your conscious mind is asleep or drugged. In daily life a dream house with this or that and the other can become a nightmare when you awake to the realities of things you have not seen.

When you have found the home you want, there is no harm in making a verbal offer to the agent. Some bargaining about purchase price is normal and expected. There is no need to feel unduly pleased if you make a quick deal and get a couple of hundred off: if you haggle a bit longer you will probably save twice as much. But don't bargain over-much if the house is just what you want where you want it, though to the agent you should expose all the shortcomings you can: you may save a hundred in two or three thousand, but if you do not close the deal you may lose what you want.

You may be asked to put down a deposit as a sign of your good faith: it is no such thing. Even if you put down a deposit, the owner can change his mind if he wants to: so don't put down a deposit. If a verbal agreement is not good enough, the deposit may merely bind you without necessarily binding the vendor or his agent: the more keen they are to sell, the more likely there is to be a catch.

So when you have agreed a price—if you do—say you will instruct your solicitor at once to confirm it. He will make your offer subject to a report by a surveyor, whom he will recommend to you, and to the final contract. In his written offer to the seller, he will repeat not only the terms of sale and the date of taking possession and other necessary details, but also any promises the agent may have made to you when trying to put the deal over. If the surveyor finds defects like dry rot or a bad roof or unsafe wiring, or if the solicitor finds that there will be heavy road charges or development plans or other similar things which will make your bargain a bad one, there will still be time to call the deal off or have it reviewed.

If anything is put into writing without a solicitor's advice, or if a deposit is paid without the receipt being clearly marked 'subject to contract', the buyer may find that he has deprived himself of any rights he may have, and unless the owner is unable to produce good title may not be able to withdraw. If he can't raise the rest of the money, he will at the least forfeit his deposit and the owner may claim for any further loss. He may even find that he has committed himself to buying a house of which he cannot get possession when he wants it.

It is always interesting to know why the owner is selling, but you do not necessarily have to believe what the agent tells you. He is only in business to make a sale and collect his commission. The protection which you, as an amateur buyer, need from a professional seller, in this, probably the most important financial transaction in your lifetime, is a good solicitor.

Chapter 3

HELPING A MAN TO RETIRE

A GREAT many men at first when they retire have a feeling
of uselessness, amounting in some cases to hopelessness, largely
because they lack enough money and interest in life and living.
Circumstances alter cases. Life is apt to be fuller and freer for a
retired person in the country than for one in a town, for one
with money than for one who only has the retirement pension.
There will always be a substantial proportion of men to whom
retirement must seem the blank wall of a dead end rather than
a turnstile into a new life: for most it is but a passing phase.

Even a husband prepared for retirement may be in for trouble
if his wife is not. A woman who is going to have a man on her
hands (and maybe under her feet) ought with thought to face
up to the prospect: in all probability she is the *only* person who
can vary it. She can never retire. Her husband's health and
happiness, and her own, may depend on her understanding of
what the future may hold, and how wisely she guides him in
the years before he actually ceases work: otherwise she may find
that when his job stops, his life stops, even though he remains
alive.

What any individual requires for contentment is peculiar to
himself. Some when they retire are perfectly happy doing as
little as possible: others say that they have never been so busy:
both sorts may be happy enough. At the other extreme, there
are always people ready to feel lonely and sorry for themselves: retirement provides an excuse for self-pity which no
one can deny to them, and which may show itself in many
guises. In between are a great many who would like some
occupation but are unable to find any or unwilling to accept
what is available.

This last lap of life is as much a part of living as any of the
earlier phases: and it can be a long one, for the chances are that
a man who reaches 65 will live another thirteen years. Most of

us, from middle-age onwards, have some pain or disability to remind us of our increasing years; yet a surprising number of people even in their 80's remain active and relatively free from physical handicaps.[1]

Since at 65 there is a reasonable likelihood of a further dozen years of life, for the average man to retire from full work at that age is sensible. To do so then allows him to embark on his new life with some chance of making a success of it. Indeed, it is a pity that most men cannot retire at 60; because 60-65 for so many would be golden years for such as wish to work out a new way of living—if only there is the money. Instead, not a few find these last few years of work stressful because the burden has become too heavy for the back. Save for a craftsman and for a few others who are self-employed or can go their own pace, 70 is usually too late to retire from a full day's work.

No one can know how many active years of life remain. But there is at least a three in four chance that if a man reaches 70 he will live more than another four years, and a one in two chance that he will survive for more than eight. There does not seem much sense in struggling on working from 65 to 70 if the remaining years in consequence are to be duller, emptier, and probably fewer. It seems a pity not to leave off whilst there is energy for finding or making new interests which can replace those of a lost job and possibly meeting new people who will become friends. As we grow older not only do we lose friends but we ourselves become less friendly.

On the other hand, if a man has no interests outside his work and is of such a disposition that he is never likely to find or make any fresh ones, he may as well go on working as long as possible (perhaps in a position of lessened responsibility or strain and with shorter hours) providing he is not a hindrance to others. We cannot argue with human nature, nor should we try to alter it: if he lives only for his work he may die when it ceases. In this he may be fortunate to be spared empty days, for there are people to whom their work is their life and to whom compulsory retirement spells disaster. They may not be interested in anything else, or after a busy and perhaps responsible

[1] See Appendix I p. 160. Health and Strength in Old Age.

life cannot turn to a new interest even if it be one within their powers and related to the old.

The really selfish elderly people are those who merely 'go slow' and neglect their responsibilities for the last few years before retirement, and the wilfully blind who continue when they should not. So often a failing person is blind to the decline in his powers—maybe can't or won't see, but anyway, doesn't. Inability to do full justice to his work, or loss of profitability in business or trading, the knowledge that his energy is waning or that his standing is declining, these are all good reasons for a man to pass over control and his responsibilities to others, even if he does not actually retire. None of us is indispensable though we like to think we are. A mature man will be interested in choosing his successor and in grooming him for the work which must, one day, be left to another. It is in such cases that usually only a woman—no matter whether wife, sister, or daughter—can assert a gentle persistent pressure with the probability that she will save his feelings from being deeply wounded or other people harmed.

Different occupational groups have different problems when they retire. Many professional men derive much satisfaction from the personal character of their work, and association with their colleagues and are stimulated by meetings and gatherings. As such a man grows older he not only has to try to fill the void caused by the loss of the occupation of his life-time, of which the fifties are usually the golden years of fulfilment and achievement, but contacts with kindred souls with similar interests also disappear either suddenly or—more usually— gradually.

For the worker in industry or business—at whatever level— retirement may bring about a more sudden change, and one out of his control. Sense of personal achievement can rarely match that of a professional man. Many feel keenly the loss of status which attached to the job they did or the position they held before retirement, knowing that they are no longer people of importance. There can be no denying that this is deflating to the ego and painful unless there are inner resources with which to counter it. Usually there is also a severely reduced income to limit social expenditure and pleasure, and the loss of an expense account with its attendant luxuries: at a different level a man may find himself unable to pay for a round of drinks or his annual holiday to Blackpool or Southend. All these are humbling and are correspondingly resented. That such a man may get things sadly out of proportion is difficult for him to grasp, nor can he readily correct the balance of his ideas. But a woman can help him merely by understanding what ails him and why, and in time he will make the necessary adjustment. In all probability the wife will feel the loss of status more. She will have to manage on less, entertain less, and uncomplainingly will have to do work which normally she would delegate to a paid help. But so many men and women, such as the paid help, have no status to lose when they grow old, merely dull poverty to face.

It is commonsense that, providing there are other interests, earlier retirement should prolong life. The people who have the longest and healthiest lives are those who are regular in their habits, calm and unhurried in their method, can and do avoid strain and tension, and have sufficient warmth and food. These conditions cannot obtain when a full week has to be worked. If men in their early fifties had to slow their pace as most women must, for at this age in fact they have passed their physical (not mental) peak even if they don't realize it, a higher proportion would live as long as their women folk. A woman cannot stop a man from driving himself, and will be unwise to dwell on his increasing years: she should let him face up to the signal that he is on his last lap when he comes to his sixtieth birthday or actual retirement. What she can do is to see that he has rest at night, that week-ends and holidays are real breaks from routine and responsibilities, and that these injections of fresh air into his later working life are pleasurable. This is more easy because, for so many, responsibility for children is a thing of the past, and grandchildren—in small doses—can be a new satisfaction common to them both and pleasant for all.

The world has no obligation to find him occupation. What— if anything—he does in retirement must rest with him. As a rule in towns some sort of part-time work is not too hard to obtain. Unless we do things with people life tends to get very narrow. If the world has no need for a man who has retired, his later years may be a burden empty of happiness.

By wise experimenting in spare time and holidays *before* retirement they can come to test new interests in places and people which may determine where they will live and what he will do and thus be of paramount importance later on. At week-ends and on his holidays if he does not stay at home he should go somewhere which suits him, and do what pleases and interests him. If he does not like travelling or visiting friends or relations, at his time of life he should not make a toil of what could be a pleasure: he may find happiness pottering in his garden or garage or fishing or playing bowls. A wise woman will encourage his likes and avoid his dislikes, and will not attempt unduly to mould or alter them or tie him to hers. This is as much in her own interest as in his. Another day, when his work is done, she will be glad to have him out of the house at times: a surprising number of poor old men are made to stay in bed on wash-days, I find as I go my rounds, simply to keep them out of the way. If both have some interests of their own in which the other does not directly share, they will have something fresh and interesting to tell each other in the quiet hours. There are elderly couples who seem wholly absorbed in each other; this is a pleasant state which another day may lead to desperate loneliness—the price, as one old man put it to me, of 43 years of happiness.

It is in their forties and fifties that the health of men in their retirement is often determined. Life should be lived, but if the strains and stresses are shifted on to younger shoulders, this will be good for both. There are many diseases we cannot avoid, but ill-health is less often a matter of ill-fortune than is generally realized.

There is one golden rule of health for all middle-aged people. It is that if something not usual is noticed, a lump or a pain or any other symptom which persists for more than a short time, or if something present for a long time changes in character, the family doctor should be consulted. So much ill-health could be prevented, and so much early disease cured—especially cancer—if only this rule were followed. There must be a reason for some unusual happening: what matters is whether the reason is important. Even if a reason is never found, it will have been only commonsense to have sought advice.

Now a wise wife who will bear this golden rule in mind (not only in relation to her husband but also to herself) and will see it is applied, if and when need arises, will be doing what she can in the most positive way possible to preserve health. She may have to overcome her own fears as well as her husband's, but this is a task for which she is peculiarly well-suited. She may almost have to take him by the hand and lead him to their doctor, but she should not flinch for she may easily be saving his life and at least no harm will come. Many non-painful diseases, which may cause varying degrees of chronic ill-health, show their presence in one or more small ways whilst they are still curable. A doctor's principal difficulty may be to determine whether the symptoms complained of are important or not: a wife should not hesitate about asking the doctor again if they do not quickly clear up, for her husband almost certainly will not. The wiser and more experienced your family doctor, the more readily will he agree that he is not infallible. But one should be as safe as is reasonable, rather than sorry because one is casual.

Many men approaching retirement are troubled because the memory will not hold matters of detail. This is often first noticed after an operation or when they have been in poor health. It is a nuisance though of no more importance than the fact that at 45 few women can thread a needle, even at arm's length, without glasses. Remembering depends first on observation or perception, then on registering this in the mind, and finally on being able to re-collect the memory from the stores in the mind. The more anxiously he tries to remember small details, the more likely a man is to agitate himself unnecessarily and so make matters worse. If he will be content to write down the minor things, he will remember the major ones well enough, though he may have to make a more conscious effort to do so than in the past. It is frustrating to forget things, and sometimes rather frightening, and it is especially important to make a written note of something to be remembered which arises when one is interrupted whilst doing something else. A wife who understands the difficulty and its naturalness, and that it arises from a lessened inclination to concentrate and to store short-term memories, can do much to maintain his confidence in himself. At 60 forgetting is far more often a sign of maturity and a full mind than of an ageing one. But it does indicate the need to review a process of thought after a lifetime of effectiveness, and to make the adjustments necessary in this as in other things.

Finally, a woman can switch on the yellow light. A man at around 60 may be well and active, and so continue for years. Some men feel they must 'keep up' with their sons: it is possible for a while, but it is not natural or commonsense; for each generation approaches its many-sided world from a different angle. Once on the other side of the hill, his path leads him to physical limitations which will not be denied and should not be ignored: inexorably, they have been coming on since he was 25 or 30, and one day they must have their way. A wise wife will remember this and will see that he does not launch into early retirement as if he had found the secret of eternal middle-age. In our later years (sometimes more readily than in earlier ones) a solution can be found to most problems save those which involve physical powers; after 25 these do not remain as they are. Around retiring age, guidance is needed by most men. A good wife will find that her influence and understanding, un-seen and unfelt but so very real, can be the guide and staff her husband—however dominant in the past—will come to depend on increasingly as the years march quietly by.

Chapter 4

KEEPING AT WORK

O L D E R workers of all classes are valuable when labour is in short supply. The worker at or about retirement age is usually absorbed when there is need, but liable to be the first to be 'put off' when demand falls away. Men who have to give up their occupations tend to lose their sense of belonging. The recipe for successful retirement that will suit one man will be different from what will suit another: many will wish to continue in some kind of occupation.

The official retirement age is not that at which a man becomes too old to work. Indeed, age would probably be considered the least important factor were it not tied up with retirement pensions. For the many who wish to continue to 'work' what matters most is that the demands of what is available should match their capacities.

In general it is more important for a single man to continue in some form of occupation than for a married one, and this is especially true of widowers, so many of whom find the loneliness hard to bear. By most men, work is desired for its own sake rather than for the money it brings in, and higher wages will usually be sacrificed for a more suitable and secure job with less pay, for profit is not as important to a retired man as to a younger. Herein lies the danger that they may be exploited by the unscrupulous.

If a man wishes to work, and suitable work is available, mere age is no bar. But not many retired people are clear about what they want to do. Not every wife likes having her man about the house for most of the day. On his retirement she may wake up to the fact that she has been a part-time wife for thirty-five or forty years, and that in fact she neither knows nor understands him very well. Such a man will be better finding himself another job than sitting at home getting under his wife's feet. Health and happiness depend on having interests and maintaining human contacts: lack of purpose and loneliness—some men are very lonely in their own homes—breed apathy, and this is a pitiable state.

A man in his middle sixties will feel strain more readily and fatigue more easily. One of my patients, at seventy, has a job as an 'Office Boy': this suits him and an understanding employer very well. But it involves his driving forty miles on country roads each day, which is hard in the winter: though he likes the work he is looking for something nearer at hand. Much the same will apply to those who have to face the rush hour on the tubes and buses in the big cities. Inability to stand such strains is a normal accompaniment of age, as is the tendency to fatigue quickly in the face of work involving physical effort.

Excessive strain and fatigue may be noticed first at the weekends, when there is such a blessed sense of relief, rather than at the day's end when to feel tired is natural. The five day week, which gives two days clear rest, enables many to keep going. But among my own patients it is generally known that men around or over sixty who do manual work, or married women, and girls in their teens, can have a week off from work on request with my blessing and co-operation: for prolonged ill-health may thus be prevented.

Men who continue to work after sixty-five are a self-selected group: the weaker brethren will have given up. Mostly they will find work for themselves which will minimise strain and fatigue—as, indeed, many do before retirement, like painters giving up ladder work. What an older man needs is shorter hours and freedom from responsibility: such jobs exist but are hard to find. We may forget, as we grow older, that simple things may become beyond us. Frequent stooping is an exhausting business: yet this is not surprising when it is remembered that in the process the top half of the body, several stones in weight, is lifted up. The work offered may be light enough, but the necessary movements may be fatiguing: standing for long periods, or work involving a good deal of walking, may tire out an elderly man. Because powers of concentration tend to lessen, monotonous work is to be avoided: and piece work is not popular with older workers because it involves a high pace of work, however simple, perhaps as a member of a group which includes younger men with whom they have to keep step. A man in his sixties in a business or a factory should be a helper rather than a producer. As a rule, their reliability and trust-worthiness can make them valuable employees.

Elderly men take poorly to shift work. The human body has natural rhythms and gets used to doing certain things at certain times: if these are varied, re-adjustments have to be made. There are tides in our bodies with which we can no more argue than Canute could. From thirty onwards, the human body func-tions less efficiently if its routines are altered, and the effects linger for a week or more. If shift work is at night, sleeping in the daytime is often difficult and the digestion disturbed. On the other hand, continued night work, or rising early as to do a newspaper round, is acceptable to many elderly workers once they get accustomed to it. At best they are likely to be light sleepers, and awaken early.

The outlook of manual workers is different from that of those who wear a white collar. For the former, if the mind is to be occupied the body must be occupied as well. Since they are in the lowest pension groups, not a few turn to gardening and keeping livestock. Many have never got through a book in their lives, and rarely read anything except a newspaper—and then only for the football or racing which give them a speculative interest. Surprisingly many dislike the radio and television, and though these are taken for granted, even those who do nothing in their spare time may find little interest in them. Not a few married and domesticated men take over the care of the home so that their wives may go out to full-time employment, and this is good for both of them.

The white collar worker in many ways is better off. He has a higher pension, more education, and naturally has more intel-lectual interests, whilst the whole field of voluntary service is open to him, if he chooses. He is perhaps more limited in his choice of what paid work he can do—the menial jobs are not for him. Intelligence tests show that in average mental agility a man in his sixties has reverted to the level of a boy of about twelve. Age twelve is not slow—parents know that it can be disconcertingly swift—and the step is compensated by a matured understanding and long experience: but it will limit his ability to venture into pastures new.

In the late sixties disease may leave marks on health and often restricts activity. Men who are content to do nothing often go rapidly downhill, whilst others who pursue activities within their capacities, seem more able to enjoy to the full the compensations of old age—a philosophical attitude arising from the capacity for serene detachment, a release from the pressures which plague middle-age, a quiet enjoyment of seeing the world as it is and not caring overmuch if it is not as it 'ought' to be.

There is a story of a man—once at the head of his profession —who before retirement promised himself that he would then do all the desired things for which he had never found time. But quite early after the event he discovered that a great part of his time was taken up with putting these things off. Eventually putting them off seemed to take up all his time. But even so he was content. He should have known: he told the story. There is a moral in this somewhere.

Chapter 5

MONEY

W H E N surveying the financing of the journey on the other side of the hill, it is well to remember that usually there are two stages in retirement. For most, the first commences suddenly somewhere around 65; the second, more complete, takes place quietly in the later years. Each has its own special problems.

Retirement is almost always accompanied by a sudden and often severe drop in income. It is difficult to have to live on half or less than half of what one formerly had, and perhaps in addition to miss benefits like a tax-free car. Early in retirement around 65 this fall in income can often be lessened by a sideline; and it is important not to mind too much if this should involve some loss of former status, because the need is not only for extra money but for occupation. It is also practical, five or ten years earlier, to start a fund to cushion against the financial shock of the event, and to this end to bank or safely invest any extra money—like bonuses, or pay rises, or capital gains and other windfalls—which may come to hand during those years when there are still earnings. This fund should be apart from ordinary savings, because it is almost certain that it will be needed. People in their fifties often find themselves with extra funds because income has risen and family expenses fallen. So it is wise to invest in labour saving devices and to replace worn linen and floor coverings, and at least to keep up the wardrobe. Later on, even necessary expenditure will be avoided when the household budget is delicately balanced. Many people nowadays contribute to private superannuation schemes which supplement the retirement pension paid by the government, and so have no pressing need to save for retirement as in the past. The most difficult period is often during the first eighteen months or two years of retirement, when adjustments are being made and possibly extra and unexpected expenses being encountered just at the time when income has been cut.

39

The second stage, usually after 75, is of more gradual onset than the first, but whereas in the earlier people may be able to help themselves in this way or that, during the later most have lost the ability to do so. By then they are almost certain to be living on a relatively fixed income; the policy of gentle inflation favoured by most governments as bringing the greatest benefits to the greatest number is likely to present problems for those least well placed to deal with them. There can be no rule to guide one to avoid this bogey, because times and the financial climate change every few months, but it may bring unhappiness and insecurity to the later years. Poverty is always a cause of unhappiness, but when it magnifies any troubles in old age it is bitter indeed: even though nowadays there is National Assistance to fall back on once savings are exhausted, so that none need feel themselves to be wholly destitute.

It is written in Ecclesiasticus, 'Better that thy children should ask of thee than that thou look towards the hands of thy children'. If you have money, keep enough under your control. This is not to say that if one dear to you is in need you should not help, if you can spare the money. Nor does it mean that you should not make gifts, if you can afford them; such presents give much pleasure especially if they are unexpected, and if care is taken not to make them as a sort of bribe or to give favours to one and so cause jealousy in another. Be wise in your generosity, or you will regret it, as may others, and keep your own counsel except from a confidential adviser.

Do not turn over most or all of your money or property to some one on the understanding that you will then be supported for life. Times and people change, and if you part with what you have there will be no opportunity to find more. Misunderstandings do not as often arise out of the selfishness of the younger generation as is imagined by those who have handed away their savings. There can be the point of view of the older person who, rightly or more frequently wrongly, may feel that he has paid too dearly for the care he is receiving: or that of the young people, who may consider exaggerated the ideas which the elder has of his 'gift' and of what it will accomplish in these days with the changing value of money. All too often an arrangement of this kind, where there is a definite promise of continued support, is the seed of a misunderstanding which can disrupt a family completely or leave the older person suffering agonies of disillusionment.

Those people who keep their financial independence retain independence in other things. They are more likely to be careful than to be generous, to have barely enough than to have too much. The best thing a man can do is for him to manage his affairs himself as far as he may; his lawyer, bank manager, accountant or the national assistance officer, should be told as much as necessary. For a woman the situation is rather different; her estate has often come to her from a husband or relative, and probably she is not used to business matters. Many sons are sensible and will give good advice without asking or wishing for control. If there is any doubt a lawyer, accountant or bank manager, being independent and impartial, will usually be a valuable help and guide.

Many elderly people are able at business, and are on the lookout for a 'bargain'. As the years go by the odds against them lengthen, and not a few have to pay to find out that they are not as clever as they thought—a lesson it is desirable one should learn before 70, for it is indeed hard to bear to be taught it at 80.

It is not easy to know how best to lay out one's money. Two childless patients bought the house in which they were living: it was cheap, but it took the whole of their savings. So they were left with only their pensions and had to have National Assistance. They would have been better advised to go on being tenants (as it happened they had complete security) and whilst they had any savings to spend them on making life easier; with the knowledge that when these were exhausted National Assistance would still be available to them. Their bargain was a good one; but it was an unwise purchase because all their spare cash was tied up—there was none left even for repairs—and so they were worse off than before. A house is not a good bargain if it will be an expense to us in our retirement.

There is not a lot of sense in leaving behind hard-earned savings for another to spend: though people who save usually find difficulty in spending. But it is foolish to have money in the bank or earning a relatively small return and to go without the comforts which can make life happier and more pleasant: one should always keep a little capital available if possible.

Another patient sold her house, and bought a smaller one. She then owned her house, had a private income of £100 a year, and also had £2,000 in the bank. To invest the latter in Defence Bonds at 5 per cent would bring her in £100 a year, and her capital would remain intact. People do not like to draw out capital, so she would almost certainly have tried to manage on £200 a year less rates, taxes, etc., by depriving herself of things which she could afford and which would make her life more agreeable. Enquiry showed that if in addition to her private income of £100 a year she bought an annuity[1] with £1,500 of her capital she would receive from it £154 a year for the rest of her life, and still have £500 for emergencies drawing £25 a year interest until she needed it—an increase in income of £80 a year.

Yet another patient—aged nearly 90—told me she had won a £500 prize* in the Premium Bonds. When I asked her what she was going to do with the money she said 'I've got a wonderful bargain. I've bought an annuity from an insurance company and I'm going to spend every halfpenny of it—not a farthing will go in death duties, and very little in income tax'. Whether or not in fact she has a 'bargain' remains to be seen but she found two new interests: one was to go on living for as long as possible to get her money's worth, the other would come from spending without a care.

Those who have saved for their old age will never lack counsellors on how to invest their money. So long as these are not trying to make your fortune for you—avoid such like the plague—they may be helpful if money is their business. To be on the safe side, before you act apply these simple rules and then

[1] See Appendix II p. 161.

* These prizes are not taxable and many wealthy people consider them to be a reasonable investment because to the heavily-taxed it is worthwhile buying a large amount (maximum is £1,000) not only because luck usually favours the 'haves' rather than the 'havenots' but if the 'draw' is impartial the interest which the prizes represent will come to them in time.

you should have no cause to regret what you finally decide to do.

1. Spread your risks: don't put all your capital into one basket. If you have money to invest, don't do it all at once but take your time even if you lose a little interest.

2. If you decide to buy securities, for the safety of your interest buy the very best shares in any group; but for the safety of your capital make your purchase when a sound share is cheap because out of favour, for you can afford to wait and in a year or two it should again be on the upgrade.

3. Never buy any securities unless they are quoted on the Stock Exchange, and only do so through your bank, solicitor or a member of a Stock Exchange.

4. For safety's sake, don't put your money into mining stocks or abroad—under the ground or over the water—except it be in large finance houses or international companies. Even industrial securities of the highest class are doubtful investments for the elderly: for the better they are the lower the rate of dividend interest, and the capital value will vary with the temperature of the financial and political climate. To a large investor this may not matter, but to a little man it may represent worry and anxiety and these are to be avoided in our later years. 'High yielders' are tempting, but not suitable for widows, orphans, and the elderly.

5. Unit Trusts are for young people rather than the elderly, except when stock markets are very depressed. The rate of interest is usually low, but though the capital value may increase it will fluctuate with the general level of the stock market. This is governed not by the real value of shares but by the law of supply and demand.

6. Because the interest rate is fixed, certain forms of security in which the capital cannot decrease in amount, and investments in Buildings Societies, are favoured by elderly people. But these need choosing with care, for none of them give any protection against the erosion of the *value* of the capital by inflation.

(I) National Savings Certificates pay no tax: the rate of interest is only 3¾% tax free. This is a good return to a rich man, who should hold as many as possible, but a poor man who pays little or no tax can do better in other fields.

(II) The Post Office Savings Bank pays even less at 2½%. The first £15 of interest is tax free, but this is of little or no benefit to a poor man. But even 10s should be shown on the I.T. Return. If the interest credited in any one year exceeds £15, this will be reported to the Inspector of Taxes. So that if several years interest is added at once because the 'book' has not been kept up-to-date, there may be a demand for tax though if the situation is explained it will not be enforced: but such a demand can be a worry in our later years.

(III) Bank deposits may pay a better rate of interest than the Post Office, but this varies with bank rate. If the interest totals more than £15 in any year this has to be reported to the Inspector of Taxes by the bank.

(IV) Building Societies pay about 3¾% tax free. This form of security also should be of relatively little interest to those who pay little or no tax. Of course, the tax element can be re-claimed, but this is not at the full rate and in any case it involves an investor in correspondence with the Inspector of Taxes: probably both are anxious to avoid this. One advantage is that to invest money in a Building Society is an easy and expense free form of investment, and the capital will usually be paid back quickly at demand.

7. For the average investor who requires reasonable safety of capital with a high fixed rate of interest which is paid before deduction of tax the two following groups of securities are relatively trouble free. As with most fixed interest securities, the capital is subject to fluctuation in value, but with these it may be either up or down.

(I) Government Defence Bonds, which must be redeemed (repaid at par) at varying dates, are important to those who pay little or no income tax as the interest is paid before tax is deducted and so has not to be reclaimed. Since they mature at varying dates, the amount of interest received will vary with purchase price: in general, it will increase in amount with each year extra before the Defence Bond matures. Capital appreciation received on redemption or on sale (if they have been held for more than six months) will be free of tax.

(II) Interest on $3\frac{1}{2}\%$ War Loan is paid before deduction of tax. As there is no fixed date for redemption, the capital value has depreciated with inflation and interest payments usually these days amount to $5\frac{1}{2}\%$ per annum or even more on the money invested. It is as trouble-free as possible for those who wish for a fixed income, though the value of the capital may vary from time to time. This is probably the best form of permanent trouble-free investment for an elderly person.

8. A rather higher return than is given by gilt-edged may be obtained by investment in the fixed interest Debentures or Preference Shares of first-class companies. A Bank or Solicitor or Stockbroker will indicate which are most favourably priced, but only those of the biggest and best companies should be bought to ensure safety of income. Tax is deducted before payment.

9. The highest possible safe income for life is obtained from an Annuity bought from an Assurance Company, but the capital disappears altogether. Married people, or two sisters, or brother and sister, may have a joint Annuity which continues to be paid after the death of one so that there is no fall in income to the survivor: the return on this is naturally rather lower than when it is on the life of one person only. There is no medical examination before buying an Annuity: but mostly they are taken out by people in good health who expect to live for many years if not forever. Nonetheless it is wise to have a word privately with the family doctor before the Assurance Company is approached. Under no circumstances should the whole of one's capital be sunk in an Annuity: for practical purposes it cannot be redeemed, and if any extra capital is required it is either not available at all or can only be borrowed at a penal premium. Further information and details about Annuities will be found in Appendix II on page 161.

Chapter 6

INCOME TAX

(at October 1964)

I T may be more desirable for a man in retirement to have some knowledge of income tax, and particularly to understand the tax reliefs he may be entitled to claim, than was necessary in those active years when P.A.Y.E. dealt with his salary in ways perhaps beyond his understanding. If he is in doubt usually his bank manager will be helpful. If there is difficulty, an accountant should be consulted. It should not be forgotten that in general Inspectors of Taxes will be found to be reasonable and helpful people, willing to guide those who seek advice. On the other hand, it is for a taxpayer subject to tax to claim every relief and allowance he can, and it is no part of the duty of the Tax Inspector to take the initiative in this. If an expense or relief is allowable the Inspector will allow it if it is asked for: these apart of course from the usual earned income, small income, or married man's allowances which come more or less automatically. In practice, whatever the theory may be, the average Inspector of Taxes will not inform a taxpayer how he can reduce his liability for tax.

The free time of the early years of retirement allows some, who can and choose, to add to their reduced incomes. On these earnings tax may be claimed if total income is sufficiently large: in theory at least, all income from occasional or part-time earnings is potentially taxable. A few transactions, or even one only, may be held to constitute 'trading', and will bring an assessment or enquiry from the Inspector of Taxes if there is personal benefit to any significant extent and if he is or becomes aware of it. It should be remembered that tax avoidance, by taking full advantage of allowances and reliefs, is legitimate: tax evasion, by concealing income and similar tricks, is not. But who would cast the first stone?

So that if any additional income is earned, the most careful record should be kept of all expenses. It may be necessary to

46

show that these have been incurred by way of trade in doing or seeking to do something, or sell something, which will add to income: it is immaterial whether or not the activity is interesting or enjoyable to the taxpayer: even hobbies may be taxable.

EARNED INCOME AND RELIEFS

'Earned' income is the profit from trading, business or employment; family allowances, retirement and superannuation pensions are considered as 'earned' for tax purposes. National Insurance sickness, unemployment, and other benefits, and sickness benefits from Provident Societies and Trade Unions etc., are not counted as 'income' and are free of tax. There is a free-of-tax allowance on two-ninths of earned income up to £4,005: beyond this sum a different scale is charged, which need not concern us here. In addition, on income whether earned or unearned, a single man or woman can claim a further £200 of personal allowance, and a married man can claim £320 for himself and his wife. Even if she is not living with him he can claim allowance if she is wholly supported by him. A single man who has less than £258 a year coming in from all sources (other than gifts) or a married man with up to £378 per annum, will pay no tax on these amounts. The tax free £258 and £378 are composed of two-ninths earned income allowance or small incomes allowances (see below) and £200 single person's relief or £320 married man's relief. A married woman who is working is counted as a single person for a married woman's earned income relief of up to £200. If she is living with her husband, and is working, since she also is entitled to a two-ninth's earned income allowance in earnings she may add to their joint income £258 before any tax is payable on her earnings. This is the case for earned income at all ages, but if a portion of the income of either is unearned (that is, comes from interest, dividends, rents, or the 'interest' portion of an annuity) then the position may be altered. That portion of a married woman's earnings which is above £258 and any additional unearned income will be added to her husband's income for tax assessment: normally he has to pay the tax on their combined incomes.

A man at any age who does work on his own behalf and is considered self-employed, may employ his wife. This is not a fiddle: he is entitled to all the reliefs he can fairly claim. But he must be able to show that she really earns, that the amount he pays her is reasonable and in relation to the work done, and that the wage is actually paid over to her as it would be to any other employee. A receipt should be obtained, or payment made at suitable intervals by cheques. The essence of the matter is that for purposes of taxation all income, including a pension, is potentially taxable and even if it is illegally obtained an Inspector will demand tax if he can trace it. If a wife in fact does work which helps her husband in his business they should seek all the benefits they are allowed.

Capital gains are taxed if they arise from the profitable sale of land which has been owned for less than three years, *or* in the case of other property, such as stocks and shares, when the disposal takes place not more than six months after acquisition. The principal exceptions are owner-occupied houses, business premises and tangible movable property. Losses may be set against gains for the year, or subsequent years, until exhausted.

SMALL INCOMES

A taxpayer aged under 65 with an income of not more than £450 is allowed to claim an allowance on two-ninths whether the income is earned or unearned but he cannot also claim the earned income allowance. There is also a reduced rate when total income, whether earned or unearned, is above £450 and not more than £680: tax is only paid on £450 plus half the surplus above that figure. These tax reliefs will normally be allowed automatically by the Inspector.

OLDER PEOPLE

If either the taxpayer, or his wife if he is married—it is immaterial which—is aged 65 at any time within the tax year (which commences on April 6th and ends at midnight on the following April 5th), an old-age allowance can be claimed on both earned and unearned income if it is relatively small. A single taxpayer aged 65 or over having less than £360 a year, or a married taxpayer whose wife is living with him who has less than £575 a year, will pay no tax. There is reduced tax in both cases for up to £130 more. For those with larger incomes where the taxpayer (or his wife if he is married) is aged over 65, he can obtain an allowance for that year of two-fifths on his or their total earned or unearned income if this is not more than £900: if it is above that total there is a lower rate of tax on the amount between £900 and £1,376. It is therefore important, if the taxpayer's age, or his wife's, is around 65, and if they have unearned income, for him to know this and to draw the attention of the Inspector of Taxes to the fact that he or his wife will become 65 on such and such a date within that financial year. From then on the allowance will be made automatically. A person who is on the 'blind register'—which includes some partially sighted people—may be entitled to certain special reliefs and should make enquiries of the Inspector of Taxes.

Where a 'retired' person finds himself with business interests, capital expenditure as well as revenue expenditure, the cost of equipment as well as that of using it, must also be looked at. The essence of the matter is that these must be wholly and exclusively incurred for the purpose of 'trade', but whilst revenue expenditure is usually wholly chargeable against profits, capital expenditure is not and any reliefs will be spread over several years. It is for this reason that on occasion it is more profitable for a business or taxpayer to rent or hire and charge all rental against income, than to buy and have capital sunk, irrecoverable, and losing interest. In general, a man in retirement should not put more than a nominal amount of capital into anything, except possibly his home, unless he has so much that it does not matter.

DEPENDENTS

A taxpayer in retirement, who has children dependent on him for support, is entitled to tax allowance which may bring his income within the range of special old-age reliefs. Where the child is below 11, this is £115, between 11 and 16, £140, and over 16, £165: but in this last event the allowance is only given if the child is full-time at school or college, or is being trained full-time for a trade or profession or vocation for a period of at least two years. In *none* of these cases is the full relief allowable if the child has a taxable income of its own of more than £115 —this is exclusive of scholarships or voluntary payments by parents or other interested people. A 'covenant' (e.g. from a grandparent) in favour of a child will be considered as income. If the annual income from this and other sources (including rebate of income tax already paid by the covenantor) exceeds £115 the parents allowance for the child will be reduced by £1 for £1 of any amount of income above that level until at £230, £255, or £280 it disappears altogether. Older children may have holiday earnings which must be counted as income.

A taxpayer may also claim a maximum allowance of £75 for each relative wholly dependent on him (this may be shared by two or more taxpayers): relative, in this context, means the widowed mother of the taxpayer or his wife, a mother living apart from her husband following the ending of a marriage, or of any relative either of the taxpayer or of his wife who is not capable because of age or infirmity of maintaining themselves. A taxpayer may claim the allowance for more than one relative in any tax year. If the relative has an income of less than £180, the full allowance of £75 may be claimed: if it is between £180 and £255, the allowance of £75 is reduced £1 for £1 by the amount the income exceeds £180: if it is £255 or above, no relief is given to the taxpayer. In these days many retired people have an older relative living with them so that this will be a helpful and important concession if the taxpayer is aware of it and makes the necessary claim.

On the other hand, if by reason of age or infirmity a taxpayer and his wife need to have a daughter to live with them, an allowance of £40 can be claimed irrespective of the amount of the daughter's income. A widow or widower can claim an allowance of £75 during any tax year for a woman who lives in the house and acts as housekeeper, providing no allowance is claimed for her by any other taxpayer.

Lump sum payments to an employee of a company on his retirement or removal from office do not attract tax if they total less than £5,000, nor do lump sum payments made because of the death or injury or disability of the employee. But pensions under a pension scheme paid by an employer to a retired employee are taxed as earned income and tax is deducted from each payment at source by P.A.Y.E. If there is any change in circumstances which reduces income—as when a house is bought out of capital or income-bearing capital is lost, reduced, or given away—the Inspector should be informed as a lower code number may be applicable and less tax payable.

Finally it should be remembered that the death of a husband or wife, particularly if the surviving partner is under 65, will alter the tax position. From the date of her husband's death, a widow will only receive the single person's allowance, and if she is under 65 she will only escape tax on the first £200 of her income: similarly a widower will lose the married man's allowance. This is one reason why an annuity, on which only the interest element is subject to tax, or whenever possible a pension under an employer's scheme, should be taken out so that the death of the husband does not too severely reduce the wife's income: similarly where two people—brother and sister, or two sisters, one of whom is working, sometimes even two friends—are living together it is often better to accept a smaller joint annuity so that the survivor will benefit. The passing years will make more and more necessary the increased security thus provided. But 'retired' women, in certain circumstances may find that even widows' benefits are taxable.

COVENANTS

Older people who pay tax at the full rate may help the younger generation by covenanting to pay a fixed sum each year for seven years or more. If the payment is to a named person, the grossed up amount can be put against surtax, and so a little reduce their own tax liability. If income is transferred from a father to his child, the father will usually continue to be taxed on the full amount. But if a grandparent covenants to make an annual allowance of £100 a year to a grandchild, for seven years, (I) the grandchild gets £100 less tax at 7s 9d in the £ which is £61 5s od. (II) if the grandchild has no other income, he can then claim the tax deducted £38 15s od). (III) since the sum is less than a child's allowance for income tax, his father will still be able to claim reliefs according to age and (IV) the covenantor will pay £100 but he himself may save surtax if the gift is to a person such as a grandchild.

FINALLY

1. Always inform your Inspector of Taxes when retirement has taken place. P.A.Y.E. is only deducted to the date of retirement, and no tax is collected on the pension and other income (except from contributory schemes where it may be deducted at source) from that date to the following April 5th. When this happens the subsequent demand may be for a painful sum.

2. Tax normally is payable each year in two lump sums. So if there have been earnings a fixed weekly sum should be set aside to meet future tax demands. A good year may be followed by a bad one during which tax on the previous good year's earnings has to be met.

3. Where income is small, and part or all comes from dividends etc. which have paid tax at source at the standard rate, this tax can be reclaimed if the inspector is informed (see p. 48 small incomes).

Chapter 7

PENSIONS AND NATIONAL ASSISTANCE

(at October 1964)

I STATE RETIREMENT PENSIONS

A MAN under 70 or an employed woman under 65 is only entitled to a retirement pension if he or she has retired or can be regarded as having retired from regular employment: but once these ages are reached there is no limit to what a pensioner can earn, and the retirement pension is not affected in any way. Men under 65 and women under 60 are not entitled to a retirement pension, but at or over these ages can claim it if they choose provided sufficient contributions have been paid.

Most people when they retire give up paid work altogether and have obviously retired from regular employment. But if they decide to retire and draw the pension before reaching 70 (65 in women) they can still continue to do part-time work. When there has been retirement from work and the retirement pension is actually being received, the pension (which is subject to income tax where income is sufficiently large) may be affected by such earnings but not by any income from rents or investments or a private pension scheme or from similar sources. The income from a book a man writes before retirement will not affect his retirement pension: but written after he has retired may do so for the number of weeks it has taken him to write it, if it is successful. The law is that earnings in any one week—however much they may be—will ordinarily only affect the pension payment for the following week. But some money may be earned in any one week without affecting the pension in the following week. The earnings rule only applies to a person who has already retired from regular employment, has qualified for his retirement pension, and is receiving it.

If a man or a woman at the minimum age continues in full work, taking the retirement pension must be deferred. When it is finally taken at or before the maximum age it will be increased by 1s per week for each 12 extra weekly contributions paid plus 6d a week for a wife aged 60 or over (who will later receive 1s a week extra to her pension for each 12 extra contributions if she becomes a widow) until the maximum age of 70 is reached (65 for a working woman). Further details will be found in a leaflet on Retirement Pensions obtainable from any Pensions and National Insurance Office.

It is important without delay to notify the local Pensions and National Insurance officer of any matters where earnings may affect the weekly pension before the maximum age is reached. Past payment of a pension cannot be reviewed to the disadvantage of a claimant unless he has not shown good faith. Questions as to benefit are decided in the first place by an insurance officer. From his decision there is a right of appeal to a local tribunal consisting of three members—one from a panel of employed people, one a representative of employers, and one an independent chairman: application should be made within twenty-one days and the local Pensions and National Insurance officer will explain the procedure. From this tribunal there is a further right of appeal to the National Insurance Commissioner who is of high legal standing and whose decision is final.

II STATE GRADUATED AND OTHER CONTRIBUTORY PENSIONS SCHEMES

The Graduated Pension Scheme came into operation in 1961. It does not apply to self-employed or non-employed people. Graduated contributions are the same for men and women and are paid by employees—including married women—on all earnings between £9 and £18 per week, and to these are added contributions by employers. The same conditions of retirement apply to the pension under the graduated scheme as to the usual flat rate National Insurance retirement pension to which it is added.

Employees who have retirement pension rights in an occupational pension scheme can be 'contracted out' of the graduated scheme by their employers if it can be shown that it is to their benefit. The employer's scheme must be financially sound, it must provide the employee 'contracted out' with retirement pension rights at least equal to the National Insurance Graduated Pension at the maximum rate, and his pension rights at least to this amount must be preserved should the employee change his job. Up to April 1962 there were some 37,000 such 'contracted out' schemes covering some four and half million employees. Both employer and employee pay a higher flat rate weekly contribution if a scheme is contracted out than when it is not.

Many employers have long been providing separate pension schemes for their employees, and the graduated pension scheme reflects in a pale way the official thought that higher paid workers should have higher pensions. Indeed, it is these schemes which are altering the general attitude to retirement, when income is not only reduced but fixed.

Each firm has its own arrangements. Many large firms have Pension Officers who will be able to give good advice from knowledge of the firm's own particular scheme: and opportunity should be sought to obtain this. On retirement, it may be possible to take the full pension, or to have three-quarters of the pension or some similar fraction and a sum of capital in lieu of the other fraction: but capital should usually only be taken if required for some such purpose as buying a house. It may also be possible for the pension wholly or partly to be joint on the lives of husband and wife, or two sisters, etc.: inevitably the pension of two will be smaller, but the survivor will be protected. The most important person a man has to consider is his wife, who should be made the beneficiary of his foresighted care. So these pension schemes should not be regarded as being inflexible. The best provide a wide variety of options such as those mentioned above, but only a firm's Pension Officer can tell what they are.

If the payment of a pension under such a scheme—often made monthly in advance—is direct to the retired employee he will from time to time need a certificate of existence: this is not necessary if it is made direct to his bank.

All pensions are taxed at source under a tax code number as

P.A.Y.E. and the tax code number is not likely to alter much in retirement. But if a retired member of a pensions scheme finds work to do he may have to pay a relatively stiff rate of tax on his earnings because personal allowances principally help those in the lower income tax brackets. This may be of some importance because if earnings after tax are small in relation to the work done, the endeavour may simply not be worthwhile. Not a few sharp people try to exploit the elderly who are seeking to earn a few extra shillings, and especially to persuade them to sink irreplaceable capital in projects which show but little return—and that poor reward often for what in fact is mere drudgery.

A man who retires at 60 under a pension scheme will not be entitled to the National Insurance Retirement Pension until he is 65: and then only in full if his earnings are less than 85s a week. But until he is 65 by law he will still be required to pay National Insurance contributions. Four courses are open to him when at any age under 65 years his pension from his firm becomes due. (I). He may go on working, perhaps in some other capacity. In this case his contributions will be continued. (II). He may be self-employed. He will have to pay the self-employed contributions himself. (III). He may be treated as a non-employed person and pay the contribution out of such income as he may have in addition to what he receives from his firm's pension scheme. (IV). He may register as unemployed and draw unemployment insurance: he then pays no contribution. When unemployed it is necessary to register in a certain trade or profession: he does not necessarily have to register in the work he has been doing, but can choose to register in the work which he wants to do, whether it is available or not. The catch here is that if no work is available of the chosen type, then after a reasonable time alternative employment may be offered and must be accepted unless it is obviously unsuitable. Much will depend on the manager of the local Labour Exchange, and it may be wise to see him before retirement or at least before registering as unemployed. Whilst unemployed he is entitled to, and will receive, unemployment benefit: this he has paid for over the years.

When a member of a pension scheme changes his job he can sometimes transfer his pension scheme rights to the pension fund of his new employer. If he does this his own contributions and his previous employer's contributions and any interest which have accumulated may be transferred in full. But if he chooses he may claim back his own contributions in the form of a cash payment. The prospect of a sum of money is always tempting, but in this instance it is plain bad business. Not only does he lose his previous employer's contributions: but no investor can hope to match the benefits paid by a pension fund. The point is made with clarity and authority in the following letter reprinted from *The Times* with permission of the writer and the Editor.

LOSS OF PENSION

SIR,—Mr. P. B. Mair (September 23), who writes that a man should take his pension with him on leaving an employer for any reason, may be interested in our experience.

A few years ago we gave this right to all our Pension Fund members, subject in some cases to a short period of qualifying service. We were told that we could not make it obligatory on a man to take his pension with him—we could not withdraw his right to encash his own contributions, leaving the employer's contributions with the fund for the benefit of the remaining members. Apart from what the employees themselves might have thought, the Inland Revenue would not have allowed us to make preservation of pension obligatory.

Our experience has been that practically every employee who has left our service has insisted on having a return of his own contributions, thus losing the benefit of employer's contributions, of interest earned and of the greater part of the tax concession.

Perhaps what is really required is some legislation that will protect the employee from himself.

Yours faithfully,
D. H. ROBERTS, Secretary, Metal Industries Limited,
Brook House, Park Lane, W.1. Sept. 25, 1963.

III NATIONAL ASSISTANCE

It is unfortunate that in the minds of so many of the older generation National Assistance is still closely linked with the old Public Assistance. There is a world of difference. Public Assistance was an indication of absolute poverty: relatives could by law be compelled to contribute to the cost of maintenance and, in general, the lowest possible amount was grudgingly given both by them and by the responsible authority. But National Assistance can be received by those who have some savings, even by those who own their own homes if they have little other income. It is a charge on the nation, and any help which is lawful will freely be given to those entitled to it. To help people who qualify for a grant is not charity but policy: because it is recognised that those who have less of the essentials than they need soon become unfit to care for themselves. Its purpose is to ensure that everyone, at whatever age, has enough money coming in each week to meet basic needs.

Until recently National Assistance did not provide very much more than a minimum of subsistence. The level has in the past been varied from time to time to ensure that a reasonable manager had enough money each week to pay for food, fuel, etc., with a small reserve for other necessities. The changes effected in September, 1959 went beyond this and not only gave to the least well-off members of the community a share in the nation's prosperity, but were a deliberate attempt to raise standards above rock-bottom.

After the payment of rent (if any) and rates, if a person has a nett income of less than the basic allowance at the time being made by the National Assistance Board, and only a limited amount of savings or investments (the house where owner occupied does not count unless some of it is sub-let) then there may well be entitlement to National Assistance. Application should be made to the local officer of the board. His address on a helpful form (O.1.) can be obtained at the local post office, as may a form (A.L.18.) which gives up-to date details of entitlement and benefits more accurately than can be done in a book of this kind. But application need not necessarily be made on form O.1.; it can be made by letter, or in emergency by telegram or telephone.

It is the duty of the officers of the board to enquire into the means of applicants, in order to assess allowances. They often go out of their way to be thoughtful and understanding of the needs of each individual: poverty is always hurtful to the feelings. No one should be afraid to apply for National Assistance, for his affairs are known only to the officers of the board, who may be trusted: there is no committee to whom they will have to be referred or detailed unless the applicant desires it. Nor should anyone be ashamed to apply: so dramatic have been the changes in the past ten years that many who had made apparently reasonable provision for retirement now find themselves hard put to it to make ends meet, with damage to their health if they struggle to do so on an inadequate income.

The amount of retirement pension varies with the age of retirement, and the number of contributions paid. But National Assistance subsistence levels are calculated *after* payment of rent and rates. There is good reason for this. Retirement pensions have to be subsidised substantially from taxation, and increasingly large numbers of retirement pensioners have savings and other private resources to supplement their pensions and bring their income well above subsistence level.

If the total income in money of a single person after payment of rent and rates or similar outgoings is less than 63s 6d a week[1], or of a man and wife after payment of rent, etc., 104s 6d, then application for National Assistance should be considered. The fact that the applicant owns the house in which he lives is not material: it is cash income in money that matters. In estimating the net income the board at present disregards any sick pay from a Friendly Society or Trade Union, or superannuation, or a charitable grant, up to 15s a week or certain disablement benefits and pensions up to 30s a week, but not more than 30s a week can be disregarded in any one case. Possession of money in cash or in the bank or building society, etc., unless it exceeds £600, need not disqualify; the weekly allowance will be proportionately reduced. But there will not usually be any reduction at all if he has less than £125 in available money, and up to £375 in War Savings invested since September 1939, is disregarded. Owner occupiers of houses are given a 'rent allowance' for rates, repairs, and any mortgage interest. It is even possible to earn a little money and still receive National Assistance, and this is important because it is such a good thing for the elderly to get out of their own homes; every case is treated on its merits, and must be discussed with the officer of the board, but it is now possible in certain cases to earn as much as 30s a week without there being any deductions because of earnings, and to keep half of the next 20s earned above 30s a week.

It is not intended here to do more than give general guidance. Anyone who is near or below the border line should apply to the local officer of the board, who will survey each case quite impartially. The grant of an allowance, however small, has become especially important since the National Health Service charges for prescriptions, spectacles, teeth, etc., were instituted. Those in receipt of National Assistance have to pay the charges like everyone else, but they may obtain an official receipt for the payment and secure a refund if they present it either when they go to collect the Assistance payment, or on demand at the Post Office.

If there are special circumstances or exceptional needs which come to the notice of the board's officer he will take them into consideration. Discretionary allowances may, for example, be given for domestic help, laundry, extra fuel, special diets, and the like, where need can be shown. The blind receive an extra allowance.

It is the aim and desire of the officers of the board to assist. To be in need, and not to obtain help when it is so easily available, is foolish: it adds an extra burden to the years, deprives some of necessary things they could otherwise have, and must lower their standards of living and health. There are those who do not realize that they are entitled to assistance: this chapter is specially intended to bring the facts to their notice, so that they may be encouraged to ask for what is available to them. People who live alone or who have to pay a high rent are the ones most often in difficulties.

The aim of this chapter is to try to make clear the principles which govern the granting of National Assistance (and of Pensions) without going too much into detail: to do the latter might easily be misleading, because each individual case has different elements. The officers of the National Assistance Board, although they are governed by regulations which have been laid down by Parliament, do not hesitate to exercise their powers of discretion in all cases where it is proper for them to do so.

But should it happen that you feel that you are not obtaining your due, there is a right of appeal to an independent tribunal if the board is notified. If you decide to exercise your right you or your representative will be invited to attend. These tribunals do not involve you in any expense. It sometimes happens that they bring to light additional facts. Even if neither you nor your representative can attend, the tribunal will examine the case with absolute impartiality and has the power to vary the allowance, but its decision is final. This is the only 'committee' which has any right to know any of your business, and then it only makes its enquiries at your request. Of course, it would be quite wrong to appeal to the tribunal unless you had good grounds for believing there to be some injustice, or that some feature of your circumstances has been overlooked. Those who are discontented with the decisions of the officers of the board usually either have some savings or accessible capital in excess of the maximum allowed, or expect the board to pay for things beyond the powers defined and given to it by Parliament. Its sole duty is to put applicants in a position to maintain a level of subsistence, and where necessary to make grants to relieve needs which if otherwise unmet might affect the health of the applicant.

Chapter 8

WILLS

All men think all men mortal but themselves
Edward Young: *Night Thoughts*

I

I T is practical to save money against the day when it will be needed in retirement; but having retired it may be more sensible to enjoy it or invest it in an annuity (keeping some capital in reserve) than to leave it for others to spend.

You may know the story of the two mourners who were coming away from a funeral, and one asked the other what he thought their friend had left: all of it, said the other, he didn't take any of it with him. There is usually something left.

It is unhappily true that the act of making a will is looked at askance by many. When you are no longer here to look after your affairs those who depend on you will be deprived of your help and support, except in so far as you have made provision for them in your lifetime. It is only by making a will that you can distribute what you have as you wish: to fail to do so, even if there is apparently only one person who can possibly inherit, may lead to expensive complications. Often people attach most value to personal things and feel they don't mind much what happens to their money or securities, but they do care who will have this piece of china or that of jewellery. In the absence of a will, your possessions will have to be distributed amongst your nearest relatives in accordance with the law, and without any regard to special circumstances or your own (unexpressed) wishes.

Whether you have much or little to leave, you should carefully consider making a will. You may not care very much what happens after you have passed on, and you may not have thought very often about the possibility of your doing so, but it will take place one day. Nothing so often arouses greed and jealousy as a deceased's estate; for no matter what or how much the beneficiaries receive, if there is any uncertainty they will usually think they ought to have a larger share. You will possibly avoid unpleasantness, and will certainly be doing your world a kindness, if you leave your affairs in order.

You can do good and give some pleasure if you dispose wisely of what is your own to leave to whom you will; much unnecessary unhappiness and distress arise because of carelessness and forgetfulness of the vagaries of human nature, but a hasty ill-considered will may be worse than no will at all.

Thought should be given to the disposal of property and money. Friends and neighbours who have been kind to you may well be more deserving of a legacy than a distant relative whom you have rarely or never seen: that a helper has been paid need not deter you from leaving a generous supplementary gift. When planning to make your will if you can recollect with gratitude the past, you will give much pleasure and you are likely to be remembered with fondness. To leave money where there has been no past service or friendship usually only invites the question 'How much?' Many people forget understanding in past years because there has been a quarrel: try not to study only today, but also to look back and remember besides your present friends those who were once your friends, even if the legacy is only a small token and reminder of happier days. Someone once said that two things which did good when spread were money and 'muck': there is much wisdom in the observation. It is always unwise to let someone know that they are remembered in your will: the knowledge may cause embarrassment, the surprise will give pleasure.

If you have any special wishes it is important not only to put them down in proper form, but to be very precise in your directions; this especially applies to furniture, pictures, jewellery, and the like, which must be so exactly described that there can be no possibility of argument. One of the most painful things we can witness is the way usually kind and generous people can fight over the estate of a loved one, and obscurity in directions of this nature has been the commencement of many family disagreements which have lasted for years and caused much unhappiness and bitterness.

Because illness or ill-health or mere age can affect judgment, it is wise to make a will before the need for it appears likely to arise. It is always possible later to add a codicil if you wish to alter it; for example someone may be specially helpful to you after your will has been made, or you may desire to encourage medical research when you fall a victim to some disease. But often it happens during a severe illness that the sense of proportion is lost and judgment clouded. Injustice is sometimes caused by over-generosity stimulated by a kind or noble thought. The importance of health cannot be overstated: none can foresee the future.

Marriage usually revokes a will previously made. It is important to draw up a new one after marriage or re-marriage or the Courts may declare an intestacy. Divorce, on the other hand, does not revoke a will; and many an erring partner has come into a fortune by the oversight of a deceased one who neglected after divorce to make a new will, or to execute a codicil to an existing will cutting out the former spouse.

When I worked in London the 'widow' of a patient asked me if I would like to buy a table I had admired when visiting him. But I never buy from patients and it was as well for they were not married, and the legal wife turned up and claimed everything. It is important that a proper will should be made where there is an irregular union, without marriage, especially as any children by it are illegitimate in law. Many of these alliances are happy and endure and often the irregularity is known only to the two people concerned. Yet neither may have a right to any part of the estate of the other except it can be shown to be a gift before death, or provision is made in a properly executed will. It may be taken almost for granted that a legal but neglected and often vindictive spouse will usually seek to obtain everything possible. If the woman dies, without specifically appointing the man to be the guardian of their (illegitimate) children, they may be taken from him: if she has made no will her child or children will probably inherit her estate which will, if they are under 21, be held in trust for them and only the income may be available for their maintenance until they reach that age. Where there is an adopted child it is important to obtain legal advice for its rights may not be those of a son or daughter. It is especially desirable in such cases to have guidance if litigation or hardship is to be avoided.

II

In England, if the estate runs into thousands of pounds, it is important for a man to make a will when there are children aged under 21 years. The law sets out to protect them against possible selfishness or extravagance by his widow. So, in the absence of a will, besides his personal things she receives absolutely only the 'personal chattels' (roughly, furnishings of the home, linen, jewellery, trinkets, and motor car) and £5,000 in cash; and also the interest during her lifetime on one half of the rest of the estate, but she cannot touch the capital (which passes to the children on her death), only the interest on her half. The remainder of the estate is held in trust for the children until they reach the age of 21 or on marriage although the interest or dividends can be applied to their maintenance. Should the wife die before the husband without making a will the same rule applies, and part of her estate over £5,000 will pass into trust for the children. The house in which the family live may be in the name of the parent who dies first and unless there is a will in which it is left to the survivor a part of it will belong to the children and when they grow up they may wish for their share in cash. Even when there are no children, if the estate is over £20,000 the widow or widower may not be entitled to the whole fortune in the absence of a will.

Where an estate is less than £5,000 in the absence of a will the whole after payment of debts, funeral expenses, death duties, etc., goes to the widow or widower. If there is no widow or widower then it is divided equally between any children, the share of any minors being held in trust: if an adult child has died, leaving children, his or her share will be divided between them and if necessary held in trust until the age of 21 is reached. If there is no spouse or surviving direct descendant of the deceased, or parents, it will go to the brothers and sisters of the deceased or to their children or in the absence of any relatives to the State: which may be unfair because the money may originally have come from the spouse who died first whose own relatives will have no rights. If the estate is a large one, it is often the practice for a husband to leave a sum of money to his wife, the rest of his estate to be held in trust for her during her life with remainder on her death to their children. By this arrangement she will receive any income from the portion which is held on trust, but when she dies there will probably be no further death duties to pay on it.

I I I

It is important that your will should be properly drawn up. Only a solicitor can be relied on to do this and I would urge you to have it done by a professional person trained to the work. Many people are shy even of making a will, much less having it done by a lawyer and paying him a fee. But you don't get much worth having in this world without a little trouble, or for nothing, as you should know by now. It is well worth the time and expense involved (as little as a guinea for a simple will) to have it done properly, and you will feel happier in your mind to know that your wishes will be carried out, and that the matter is settled and in legal shape.

Will forms are obtainable from most stationers, and if the instructions given with them are carefully followed the will should be legal. But it is very easy to overlook some small but vital detail which will invalidate the will; then your wishes may have to go for nothing and be ignored. There are legal points, which easily escape ordinary people like us. Besides, in a home made will your wishes may seem quite clear to you when you write them out, but not to whoever has to administer your estate for this must be done in a strictly legal way. In consequence, a legacy may become void because of obscurity or your intention may be misinterpreted. It is much easier for this to happen than you may think.

If your wishes are very simple, remember that it is perfectly legal for you to draw up the will yourself provided it is properly witnessed and dated. This may be more satisfactory than using a printed will form, but if a printed form is not used the will *must* contain an attestation clause to say that it has been properly witnessed.[1] Be careful to use the speech of everyday life and not legal jargon or legal terms.

IV

There is one final point. Should you desire to be cremated, or buried in some special place, or if cremated your ashes disposed of in some special way, see that your family are aware of your wish. If you write it into your will, it will be the duty of your executor to see that your intention is observed. It is important that the person you have named as your executor is aware of your desire that he should act, is willing to do so, knows that there is a will (though he need not be informed of its contents) and also where it can be found. Either the original will, or a copy, should be kept by you for reference.

[1] See Appendix III (p. 164).

Chapter 9

MARRIAGE AND COMPANIONSHIP

T H E adjustments which married people have to make when the husband retires may be more difficult than those necessary in the early days of marriage: moreover they will need to be repeated during years in which there may well be more changes than in the thirty or thirty-five when he was going out to work each day.

Retirement is the acid test of a wife: and often of a marriage. It may mean sacrificing routines, sometimes, and making up lost hours later. It will often mean having the man about the house, having more meals to prepare and to share with him— but one good cooked meal a day, besides breakfast, is plenty. A wife must be ready to let her husband do things—his ways will not be hers—and help him to feel that he is being useful. She should not let him think more often than is necessary that he is in the way: it is his home as much as hers, and his enjoyment of it now be more than he has ever had.

In most marriages the man is the dominant partner: but retirement is an equalizing process. Its commencement presents him with a very good opportunity gently to start turning over a few new leaves: these may be essential for happiness for both. He must take care not to challenge or too frequently to disorder his wife's domestic ways and plans—except to take her out: he must accept her views on domestic tidiness, spring cleaning, and the like: he must not get under her feet too much. Now that she, too, is growing older and slower, she will reasonably expect him to help her with the heavier or duller chores. He should have time, and may feel a nuisance lounging about, so he should take to himself certain jobs his doing which will make life pleasanter or easier for her. With the more limited income of retirement, part-time work, for one or both, may help. But a man's chief contribution to the home may well be his care for his vegetable garden, if he has one, (he should get mechanised

68

early) and perhaps in having a few hens: not only is there better food cheaper, but if the man produces and the wife cooks and both eat, then sharing has reached a high level indeed. An allotment can be a great help, because not only will he grow things but he will meet kindred souls who will stop him from working too hard: unlike a garden, when he gets old and feeble he can just give it up.

Companionship is the essence of marriage in the later years, but this does not mean sitting in each other's pockets. Some wives or husbands resent their partners having other interests. This is usually because one is lonely, and not unreasonably expects the other to fill the gap. Interests will narrow and diminish with the passing years, like friendships, so more and more they will come to share each other's company. If one tries to stimulate the conscience of the other by claiming to be neglected, there may be a response to the plea, but the seeds of future disharmony may have been sown and in time there will be regrets. It is usually wiser quietly to find or make one's own interests if the other's cannot be shared. It is especially true in retirement that husband and wife should show to each other the gentle manners which they would to a dear friend.

As I look back on the many elderly couples who have become old together, and whom I have known for most of my professional life, it seems to me that their later years together can be the most satisfying and even the happiest. After thirty years or more, if affection endures, two people should have sorted and smoothed out the differences of their natures, and have much in common on which to look back and to talk about. Unless there is a wide disparity in ages, their sexual relationships will have settled themselves. Some will persist even into quite advanced years, for in fact there is no time limit to intimate experience after decades of harmony and understanding; but in most cases it will quietly have faded out.

In the later years the past should be put into its proper perspective and its problems, now no longer active, not allowed to be considered important. A partner who still feels the pain of a long-ago wound should give thought to motes and beams, for this helps one to keep a sense of proportion. Two people who have lived together for so long should not find it difficult to make the most of what they have in common, and the least of their differences. For the years which stretch out ahead, and in which they will increasingly come to depend on each other in health as in sickness, need both tolerance and understanding. If affection is sour, they will be like the old couple of whom the husband said, 'Her sits on one side of the fire, and I sits on the other, and there we sits, *'ating* each other'.

Throughout this book I have tried to define a few guiding principles and then leave it to any reader to apply them as seems fit. Most elderly couples seem content: certainly to a doctor they present few emotional problems. It is not only that they have been able to adjust their ways of living to harmonize. It is not only that they have more time for leisure and thought, and have found a sense of calm and freedom. Even in the humblest cottages—this is one of the times when money does not count—many have also experienced that feeling of fulfilment, of satisfaction with life, of having had a full share of the things which really matter, which can be the priceless experience of the later years: which, when the time comes, makes the transition from this world to what is hereafter so simple, so natural, leaves so little to be regretted.

II

People who are self-sufficient will rarely be lonely however much alone they may be. Those who have been bereaved, especially widowers, are rarely self-sufficient however occupied they keep themselves, and especially in the long evenings feel loneliness deeply.

There is a great deal of happiness to be obtained from a thoughtfully chosen partnership late in life, especially for people in the fifties or early sixties: whether it be in marriage, or by two people arranging to share a home. There are many women who should have married earlier in life: but for some reason or another did not, yet have not allowed themselves to become soured or narrow. These have often much to give, for many of them have broad elastic minds, and have seen so much of the world that they make admirable and understanding companions either for a man or for another woman. The failure of a previous marriage should not deter a woman from marrying again.

Rapidly disappearing is the unmarried daughter who stayed or was kept at home, and whose mind in consequence had little chance of widening itself. By nature so often she is kind and gentle and generous. Companionship for her in later life calls for the most careful thought, because she never knows when to draw the line and to stop 'giving', for in this way she expresses her suppressed maternal instinct. But she may find late marriage to be a poor substitute for her freedom, because most men are demanding creatures: even 30 years too late, she will still wish to feel a wife rather than a mother or nurse. It will usually be wiser if she works as a housekeeper.

A woman knows what she wants to make of a man. In taking on one who is middle-aged or in the later years she is having a ready-cut or second-hand article she will not be able to alter much. Yet there can be much happiness for both parties if two people in their fifties or sixties set up house together: when one is near or over 70 the dangers increase and a permanent arrangement needs a good deal of looking at before it is finalized. Sexual relationships will be on the wane if they are desired at all, and rarely come into the picture as an important factor: but if marriage is contemplated there should be a clear understanding about this beforehand. It is a matter so many are sensitive about, especially those who have not been married before, but this should not deter them, as adults, from sensible discussion.

The essentials to be looked for are compatibility and mutual liking: next, similar social and personal standards and tastes; given these, minor likes and dislikes will usually sort themselves out with goodwill. People are pretty set in their ways by the time they reach 40, and few will change at all when they get to 70, for by then there is not the adaptability of early maturity. If two people in their later years like each other and are thinking of marriage for the sake of companionship, it may be commonsense for them to share a home together for a while before finally committing themselves, and one giving up completely the former way of life. The difficulty is that the world tends to base its ideas of moral conduct in these later years on what is fairly and reasonably expected of younger people, to whom sexual relations have an altogether different importance and significance. Many would be more sure of finding lasting happiness if a trial at this age were recognized as being sensible, and that the question of morals hardly arises.

One frequent obstacle to the marriage of people of mature years is the attitude of their adult children. Socially it is no business of the latter, nor is it any reflection on a dead partner if the survivor marries again—indeed, if anything it may be a compliment. Where money comes into the picture, sympathetic consideration ought to be given to the rights of near relatives who may feel they have an interest which they are in danger of losing. The essence of the matter is to do what is fair to all parties, even if some have to wait; and the whole thing should be settled before one becomes too old to care. Money rarely brings happiness or much pleasure in our later years, only a measure of security. When both parties have some, whether they marry or merely share a home in later life, their estates may just as well be kept separate. It may be sensible for each to make a will leaving a life interest (in the home, at least) to the other, so that ultimately any capital will come to children or others who have reasonable expectations.

III

Most of what I have written above with regard to marriage will also apply when relatives or friends of the same sex are thinking of living together and through companionship meeting their decreasing capacity to live independent lives. In such an arrangement even more care is necessary that standards and tastes should be nearly matched, and liking mutual, and that there is an absence of the little things which irritate.

No arrangement of this kind should be entered into until it has been given a trial. Staying together may show up difficulties which had never been thought of. If one or more short holidays do not demonstrate any obvious snags then a longer trial period, say for two or three months to last until the novelty has worn off, is worth the expense of keeping a flat or house of one unoccupied for a while, unless there have been sufficient contacts in the past to make it probable that personalities will not clash. Either party should be able to withdraw without giving explanations and without too many hurt feelings.

Some women can never live with another woman: often they have been married and are accustomed to a man about the home, others by nature prefer to be on their own. A tidy woman cannot live happily with an untidy one, a domesticated with a casual one, and few people can live with a dirty one. A housewifely woman will make allowances for a man and tidy up after him: but usually she can neither understand nor accept a woman whose ideas differ greatly from her own and it is no good pretending otherwise. Few women over 70 are likely to link up happily together: usually they are better and happier on their own. But if one is a paying guest the relationship is altered and there may be more chance of making such an arrangement a success; at any age we prefer to drive rather than be driven, unless we are paying the coachman.

Some time ago I knew two sisters, both in their seventies. The older, a childless widow, had lived quietly and alone for many years, and was going blind. The younger was single, had enjoyed a full life, liked people, and the intention was that she should give up her rooms in London and come to the country where they would live together. As my contacts with them grew, my doubts mounted. The younger was not merely going to have to face uprooting from her own home and losing all her friends, but to change from the complete freedom she liked to being tied, perhaps for the remainder of her life. They seemed to me, though sisters, to have little in common: and the older was taking her blindness badly, for the words 'I wish' were never long off her lips.

I worked on them gently, and in the end the older went into a Home for the Blind, the younger back to her flat and friends clear in her conscience that the wisest course had been followed. Village doctors like myself live very close to our patients,

73

and I know just how much unhappiness may be the reward of kind men and women who desire to help those to whom they are related or friendly.

To have been members in childhood of a happy family should be a substantial foundation, even after many years of separation, for an understanding companionship in later life. But it is easy to forget that all people have human faults and failings which show more clearly when they are old: however close the relationship, yet they may be comparative strangers if their ways of life have been apart. It has been said that to have friends one must be willing to be a friend. It is equally true that for common blood to have any real meaning two people must also have a good deal in common in their ways of living and thinking.

The following letter from a reader aged 73 seems worth quoting in full:—

A Country Doctor
Author of Facing Retirement

Jan. 1st, 1961

Dear Sir,

I would like to thank you for your book.

I looked eagerly to see if you had any advice for two old women living together. It is not easy for 75 and 71 year olds to adapt themselves to one another's ways, though the arrangement may be financially and in many other respects advantageous to both. It is particularly difficult if one is by nature orderly and the other not. Again, as George Eliot points out, 'a difference of taste in jokes is a great strain on the affections'. And the fact that the two may have had an amicable hostess-guest relation does not necessarily indicate that a change over to a permanent home-mate relationship will work smoothly. It is astonishing how two well-intentioned old women can irritate one another by trivial differences in their method of cutting up a loaf, using or not using a plate-rack, etc. Again, liking or not liking television or sound radio can be a source of constant friction. Indeed I have known one linking-up of two old women to come to shipwreck because one liked Mrs. Dale and detested the Archers and the other enjoyed the Archers and was bored by Mrs. Dale. (There was much *less* strain in this case from one being R.C. and the other C. of E!).

It is terribly easy for one or both to become 'catty' and for the two to settle into a state of what has been called 'intimate hostility'.

May I suggest one or two points which might help readers of a second edition of your book? Before joining up *make sure* (1) that you will laugh, chuckle, or smile at the same jokes, (2) that you have roughly the same standard of what is mean and what is generous, (3) that one is not conspicuously more fastidious than the other (e.g. over leaving false teeth in a shared washing basin.) (4) that you are both determined not to let the sun go down upon your wrath. (But not necessarily to say anything about it. It is so fatally easy to let a 'but' creep into an apology.)

It is clear that in a Home there will be more choice and variety of companionship than in a ménage-à-deux though a Home can never be as satisfactory as a four-feet-on-the-fender relation when the four feet are owned by people who have a genuine respect and affection for one another.

Grace before meals if said with honest intent can, I think, make a perceptible difference. But, of course, *both* must be able to feel that a shared meal is a bond.

It can be a tremendous help, of course, if it is possible to make two bed-sitters and if both old people share Dietrich Bonhoffer's opinion that 'solitude can be as refreshing as a Turkish Bath'.

For years I believed that I could never share a kitchen even with a saint—that it must take *two* saints to share a kitchen. But I have come to realize that even two sinners *can* rub along together not too hopelessly if neither expects more perfection in the other than in herself.

Wills. . . ! Yes, indeed. How often where there's a will there's a wail, but where there's no will there's a worse.

These notes are very scrappy and hastily written. Forgive me. But you invited letters.

Yours gratefully,

Any individual's experience must be limited. I urge those who may be thinking about marriage or sharing a home to seek out a sensible and independent adviser before they commit themselves: and whilst not delaying too long, not to hurry. Above all do not be swayed by emotion, especially pity, against one's better judgement: the first essential is mutual liking.

Chapter 10

THE ELDERLY GUEST

I

MORE and more people are living to become great-grand-parents. Not only is the number of those who reach the eighties increasing, but people are marrying younger, and finish having their smaller families some seven years earlier than was the case thirty years ago. This means that it is now relatively common for four generations to be living. One of the solutions of the difficulties caused by the increase in the numbers of the old will be their care by adult children who have themselves become grandparents whilst still in the forties or early fifties. Increasingly a complicating factor in the years around retirement of many will be the presence in the household of an aged or ageing person.

Few adults can remember enough of their own childhood, adolescence, and early man or womanhood to be reliable guides to their children as they grow up. This in itself is no bad thing, since more is learned from experience than from advice, and it stimulates each generation that it must tackle its own problems. But if it is difficult for parents to recall enough of the past to help them to understand their children, how much more difficult must it be to understand an older generation, whose voyage of discovery is in waters of which one can have had no experience at all?

The fixed groove of old people continuing to live in their own homes is often difficult for the middle-aged or elderly who go to live with and care for them. It is usually wiser for the home to be that of the middle-aged. An exception would be where an old person with failing vision is still active, because much independence can be retained in blindness if there is familiarity with the exact position of things.

Many kind people, following a bereavement, urge the remaining partner to live with them. Any pressure may be unwise. Unless feeble, older men and women may be happier with fewer material advantages than in better conditions where they are required to conform with a mode of life which is strange. Besides, it may be distressing for an old person to move in with others and to have to depend on them.

If an old person comes to live with relatives, or if they go to live with him (or her) in order to care for him, there must at the beginning be some sort of plan. Ageing people may try to dominate because they are accustomed to so doing; if this is allowed to happen the home will deteriorate. A set of firm rules should early be established, for later it may be difficult to make changes without upset. An old one needs a corner of his own, and to feel that he is wanted, that he is a part of a family which takes an interest in him; if he can do a little to help, not only will filial duty be fulfilled but he will find happiness quite un-obtainable from any other source. In tens of thousands of homes there are aged people who are content, and their families are pleased to have them.

He should have a bed-sitting-room, or bedroom and sitting-room of his own, where his privacy will not be unnecessarily invaded. A downstairs bed-sitting-room is often convenient if there is room to spare, and makes for easier working, especially in ill-health. Thought should be given to whether the stairs are too steep or too many, and any difficulties of getting to and from the bathroom and lavatory. Any one of these may present an insuperable obstacle. No old person should share a room with a child except for a very short period whilst other arrangements are being made. If there are children at school they should not lightly be deprived of the room they use for study-ing or their friends. The proposed arrangements must be fair to all. It is often desirable that the main part of the family should have breakfast alone, either by having the older person wait until later, or by taking the meal to his room on a tray.

He must have a little money of his own, and be free to spend it as he chooses. It may help him to be reminded of occasions like family birthdays and perhaps to buy small cards or gifts, though let him send them off: if he can do all this himself, so

78

much the better, for it is stimulating to him to think of others, and he can find much pleasure in so doing. Older people—by giving—will be less harassed by the need to feel grateful to the younger: gratitude is an odious burden to many. He ought to be free to choose his friends, and to entertain them occasionally and also to select his own doctor, parson, and so on, because they may seem to him to be more understanding; apparently small matters such as these may make all the difference to any relationship with him. Equally, those who care for him must be free to entertain their own guests, and to enjoy each others company and other interests without his always intruding. Because differing ages have differing tastes, things like the wireless or television programmes must be subject to some sort of agreement.

Those who have the care of an old person, still more of an aged one, should not only have a holiday whenever it can possibly be arranged, but should also get out or away for a few hours each day. Practically all aged people unless confused can safely be left for a while. The most constant attention will not prevent accidents—witness the number which occur in well-staffed hospitals. It is justifiable to take a small risk from time to time if by so doing the health and happiness and welfare of those who care for the old one are preserved. As one of my patients once said to me about her father, a nice harmless old man who could do little for himself, 'I'm glad to have a job to go to, to get me out of the house a couple of hours a day. Fair wears you out to have him repeating himself all the time. Tell him something and he's forgotten it the next minute though he can remember what happened donkey's years ago as well as anything.' She was a kind soul, and sensible as well, and I think did more in the long run because she kept a sense of proportion; not letting her emotions govern her actions though some who did not understand her difficulties might have thought her hard.

What many old people also need when they live with others is an understanding friend in whom both parties have confidence, like the doctor, parson or nurse. They can smooth out many difficulties which are brought to them because they can see both sides of the problem. It is not the least use shutting our eyes to unpleasant facts: what we must do is to face them. Such a mutual friend will help us to do so, but he must know and understand all aspects of the matter, and be familiar with all the circumstances.

The continuous strain on the housewife or family caused by difficulty in getting away for a holiday may come to a head if there is mental or bodily deterioration. So often it happens that a relative will cheerfully face carrying on her self-imposed task in perpetuity if only this can be arranged. It is a pity the authorities do not more adequately try to assist those who are carrying a burden of care which is recognized as being a public responsibility. It is to be hoped steps will be taken to ease a problem which can only grow as the number of aged people increases, for great age brings with it a disproportionate increase in defects of mind and body.

II

Whilst in our retirement we may have an older person to live with us, the order of things may be the other way round and we may go to live with others. One cannot too soon begin to think about this if it seems at all likely that it will become necessary.

The older we get the more set we become in our ways. For a man of 65 to go to live with others is more likely to be success-ful than for one of 75; both will need to be reasonable and to accept as gracefully as possible the considerable change which must necessarily take place in status within the family. On the other hand, providing it is not too long delayed, a woman should tend to defer giving up her own home because it is never easy for her to fit into that of, perhaps, a daughter who not many years back was an inept pupil leaning on her mother's counsel. At 65 a woman will be liable to be overhelpful; it will probably be wise, unless there is enough work in the home for two, for her to get a little job which will take her out for a few hours each day and so leave the mistress of the household on her own. Where there are no children, it may be practical for the older woman to see to the home whilst the wife goes out to work, but she needs must remember that it is for her to keep to the latter's method of working and not try too obviously to run it her own way however much more efficient she may think it to be. That is tactful and wise. When you are living in the home of another you will need both tact and wisdom if you hope to be truly happy and then you will also be a dearly-loved blessing.

If there are growing children, the longer a grandparent has been a member of the household the better will the grandchildren accept him or her as a part of the familiar domestic scenery. The relationship of young children to a grandparent or older person who comes to live in the home can be pleasant for both: but, especially with adolescents, the youngest generation not infrequently dislikes the presence of a newcomer. This resentment is in fact only likely to happen if they are relative strangers or if the presence of the older person causes inconveniences to the young as, for example, when there has to be sharing of a bedroom or the parlour has to be used as a bed-sitting-room. It is the home, when all is said and done, of the child or young person. The possibility must be remembered because dissention is caused in a number of families, and, in a small but definite proportion, considerable harm.

We all need the security of a home, with the possessions which are so valued by us because of their associations with the past . . . and the happier part of the past at that. The help we desire at any age will if possible be that of our own family; when we are old the simple weakness which shows itself and increases with the years is inevitable, as is an increased liability to frailty. What we require is to exercise our human and natural desire for freedom of mind and movement for as long as possible, and to continue to be part of and have a place in the world.

The final decision as to what we do ought to be ours if we are old. It is unwise for two generations to try to live together if there is known dislike or incompatibility. Even if the situation seems promising it is desirable to have a period of trial for a few weeks or months before the older person finally gives up home: the expense is always justified. Blood may be thicker than water, and kinship carries responsibilities which are often accepted, but the result can easily be an unworkable plan and prolonged unhappiness for all concerned. Happiness or unhappiness resulting from a well-meant arrangement will usually depend on one or more of four things—growing children, enough space, a fair arrangement about money, the degree of health or ill-health and the amount of time and work and tie they will entail.

Before beginning the experiment—for such it always is—if these points are quietly considered there should not be too much difficulty in deciding whether it is certain to be a failure, or whether success is possible. When there is a doubt there must be left a way to guard against failure. Good intentions are to be admired, but are no substitute for reason or commonsense.

It has been observed that where there are difficulties, friction, or conflict, these do not usually commence at the moment parents themselves begin to be dependent: there is a chain of events in which this is only the last link. The situation unless calmly thought out may have appeared to be satisfactory, but when there is a disturbance in the normal order of things the cracks begin to show. Many people are better off in a Home than continuing to live in an atmosphere of strain, and will thrive in the company of others like themselves, whilst retaining family ties previously in danger of snapping.

When we live with others the loss of the former leading position within the family group is one of the greatest deprivations we have to face. Few parents find it easy to accept a situation in which an adult son or daughter does not still need their guidance; but there has been so much change during the past twenty to thirty years that it is difficult for an elderly person any longer to be the social adviser to the family at large. We encounter the problem of the force of changes in a changing world meeting the obstacle of the methods and practice of a long life; one or other has to give way. It is usually wise for us to do so, even if we know ourselves to be right. If the lesson of the two bears —Bear and Forbear—is remembered: if the new position of relative inferiority can be accepted: if so far as may be we live our own lives without being exclusive, and without resentment but rather as interested observers will allow ourselves to be guided by those who have matured under the guidance of our generation and who have now assumed our former place in the world: then there may be much happiness for us.

If this is your new life, try to have your own interests inside and outside the house, and get out all you can to see your own friends so that your family will know you are not at a loose end. Do what you can to help in little ways, and if there is a corner you can fill, offer to fill it. Be willing, better still be known to be willing, so that you will be asked to help if need arises: but never push your willingness or weary by continually expressing it. Do not feel too disappointed if your help is not invited, or if some job you have made your own is taken away from you.

Keep up your personal standards, and dress as well as possible for the sake of those who have to live with you. With many people health is almost the only topic of conversation, and silence is better: it is a very tedious and dull subject to which to have to listen.

We should study in the years before retirement the way we must behave towards kith and kin when we are older. Those who are not yet old will be loved and respected and more affectionately regarded if they will let others live their own lives and make their own mistakes with only understanding and affection. This is but wisdom, for advice which is not sought is advice which is not desired, and there may well be rejection of the advice and resentment against the adviser. Passively, by the example of our lives and living, we can greatly but unnoticed influence others. Here indeed can be usefulness, if when we are elderly we can school ourselves to recognize that decisions can not often be ours, but that we can unconsciously stimulate thought before they are taken. When we are old, if we are sweet apples, not wormy, not dry, not sour, someone will find us out, will want us for what we are, and may be the better for knowing us.

The difficulties of an elderly or old person who lives with others may stem from several causes, and one of these is money. It is important to err where possible on the side of generosity. Contributions to the family exchequer should be regular and if enough is retained to pay for necessaries like clothes and tobacco and little presents, a person who has but a small income is making a just offering. If income is very small, it is sensible to increase the contribution by drawing on any savings he has. No one likes to feel himself a burden even though few families would look upon it in that light.

It is unwise, and unfair to the younger people, to contribute only a minimal or nominal amount for maintenance with a promise of a legacy to compensate. Such an arrangement is not uncommon, and usually someone has some regrets. For one thing there is no security; and an elderly guest may bounce off in a temper, forget to make a will, or make a will which in all the circumstances is unjust. It is in fact unfair to the elderly person also, because always at the back of the minds of both parties will be the knowledge that the 'expectations'—however well-deserved—can only become realities after his death.

If you do something for your children—now, I mean, I am not thinking of the past, nor should you—and you let them do something for you, it eases the burden of anyone feeling too much under an obligation. All one way or the other leads to disharmony.

Pay as you go, as generously as you can, and your continued presence is likely to be desired even if it may cause inconvenience and extra work. Times change, and the value of money changes with them. A pensioner probably need keep no more than 10s to 15s of his pension as pocket money but if he has enough savings and can give practically the whole of his pension or assistance in return for care it will not be too much; those who are better off can and should pay more generously. These things are always embarrassing, so in doubt a friend of both parties should be consulted—doctor, parson, lawyer—and asked for an opinion. But subject to keeping capital under control the guiding principle should be 'How much, whether they want it or not, can I fairly give to these good people who are sharing their home with me?' A rough and ready guide to the sensible *minimum* is the retiring pension, as fixed from time to time, less about a quarter.

But what, you say, if this arrangement does not work, or if I become a burden? You will then be well advised to have a word with someone whom you can trust; they will guide you, for it may well be that you will be better off living elsewhere. I wrote earlier that we all desire to retain our freedom of mind and movement for as long as possible, and few of us are so placed that we have not the right to decide. Naturally, any change must be carefully considered. But if it seems to you after seeking advice that you are imposing a burden which is not fair to ask another to bear, or if you are not happy for some reason, then a change possibly to a hospital or a home for the elderly may be the happy solution to your problem—which is also the problem of those who care for you.

Chapter 11

LIVING ALONE

I

S O M E people prefer to live alone, for it can be a simple exist-ence, with no responsibilities to others and only themselves to please: they look forward to a retirement when they will have a small place of their own, and freedom to do as they choose, and for many the anticipation will be realized. Others may feel out of touch with their friends, or elect to live by themselves lest they be a care or because, having had households of their own, they cherish an independence which they fear to lose. Yet others by bereavement have little choice, and have to work out a philosophy of accepting the limitations of living alone as best they can; there may in time be much happiness for those who find the strength to do so.

People who are not irked by solitude are fortunate. There is a great difference between loneliness and aloneness. The former begets many temptations: not least the sense of not being wanted or needed which is truly hard to bear and tends to warp one's outlook on the world. But aloneness may be rich in peace and joy. One can be very lonely when part of a crowd: and alone without being lonely. Living alone is a manner of life calling for great trust, but should imply a willingness later to accept community life if need be; to their great surprise many who do make this change find a new happiness, even though it involves the loss of the privacy previously considered essential.

People of advancing years tend to be casual about meals and appearance. The ones who live by themselves have on the average a lower standard of living than those who share a home. Equally, personal appearance must have care, for it is all too easy not to bother, and to let difficulties triumph. Some may think age to be an excuse, but in truth it is never a reason for

86

casualness: much depends on the self-discipline practised early in life.

It is important to keep active in body as in mind, and the two in fact go together. The happiest people are those whose days are too short no matter how they occupy the time and no matter whether they go out and about or whether they live largely to themselves. Some are unable reasonably quickly to do what they wish because of ill-health or pain. So in the early years of retirement the lower limbs should be studied for a little thought can often prevent or diminish future disabilities: these are mostly caused by painful conditions which will lessen mobility like arthritis of the knees or feet, corns, thickened toe-nails, bunions and the like.

Sight and hearing are of special importance, and the help which is available ought not to be neglected. Most people need glasses when they are past 60. Those who are largely house-bound and with impaired sight are unable to sew or read, are indeed unfortunate. It becomes more and more difficult once 60 is passed to accustom oneself for the first time to glasses, dentures and hearing aids, so if needed it is better to get them early rather than to defer doing so until later.

It was for some years my privilege to attend a remarkable lady who had an 'eye' for the beautiful. She lived alone in a little cottage with a small garden in the middle of a village, and her home was stuffed with good furniture and china. One day I went in and found all her tea-sets and the like had been put away. She had dropped a valued if not especially valuable saucer, through clumsiness unnatural to one who had been handling cherished things all her life: so the rest had to be placed in safety. She could not bear to part with the treasures, each with its history, which had given her so much pleasure; but she felt she had a duty to preserve them for someone else to enjoy another day. However wisely we look to the time when we will retire, we cannot plan *closely* for what may be fifteen or twenty years ahead, nor should we seek to do so, because things alter in ways we cannot foresee. My old friend, I am sure, never thought there would come a day when she would have to put away her precious china, or let her garden become a wilderness because she could not afford to pay to keep it up. But she was moderate, and enjoyed them whilst she could, and when they passed she still found pleasure and happiness in the lesser things of life, and in her friends and neighbours.

It is important, for those who live alone, quite early in retirement and whilst still fit and well, to have a little help with the heavy work, perhaps once or twice a week for an hour. Gradually this can be increased to an hour or two most days as the years pass: because it will then be more difficult to accustom oneself to start having people doing things for us. Those who are entitled to a free Home Help should ask for one: otherwise they should pay. It is a great stimulus to have someone coming in each day to do some of the work, to help to prepare the midday meal, and to tell some of the news of the world.

If physical strength begins noticeably to fail it is only sensible to conserve it, not to overtax it, and to seek and accept such help as is needed: thus retaining a degree of independence, even if a diminishing one. If we reach a stage when for one reason or another we are unable properly to look after ourselves, in our own interests and for the peace of mind of those who care for us we must be content, hard though it will seem to be, to go to some place where we can be properly cared for.

II

In the later years we reap what we have sown earlier in life, and as always at harvest time there is little we can do to increase what will come to store. If it is a poor crop, there is no obvious chance of a second one.

When we live alone there will at best be a large portion of the day when we are on our own with only our thoughts for company: at worst, it may be nearly always. But from the beginning of time men and women have sought and found in solitude a great opportunity. In these later years aloneness will be thrust upon many of us; if we can bring ourselves to accept it, our lives and the lives of those near to us will be altered. When we pass middle life we begin to measure our faith. Aloneness

88

offers great opportunities for kindly thinking and prayer, though it is for contact with real live persons that we crave, and to pray in solitude often requires much faith.

If we can and will turn our thoughts outward from ourselves, our difficulties, our loneliness, and our discomforts and anxieties, we will be happier; and others will be helped by our goodwill. If we can realize that we are lonely merely because we forget that we are not alone, we will become aware of watchful, interested, loving companionship.

Even if our bodies are handicapped and weak, as we grow old our spirits can become more free because we have more time to think. Whatever our views on religion and on the after-life, we can read the Bible: especially the Gospels and the Psalms of David—David knew life and temptation, and cried out for help in a way the elderly can understand. Then whatever our beliefs or disbeliefs, we can find comfort in our loneliness, strength in our weakness, and guidance in our difficulties. The time is ahead, perhaps, when it may not be easy to see to read the Bible: then the remembered passages of the Gospels and Psalms will still be at our disposal for meditation.

Prayer may not come readily to us, but at least we can turn our thoughts towards others and wish them well: bodily and even mental frailty is no bar to effective prayer for their needs. By our approach to difficulties, those of another generation may find strength to face their own problems. In our back-water, looking on the river of the world going by, we have the chance quietly to practise love and fortitude. If we do, our influence and the memory of us will linger sweetly long after we are gone. Kindness now which calls for thoughts and effort is the best way to atone for the small value we may have set on the virtue when we were young; he who gives pleasure is as charitable as he who relieves suffering.

No one of us is really alone, no one of us is really forsaken. Life has an unknown end for each to pursue who will. That end will probably never be revealed but still we shall have made our offering if we cultivate the land and sow the seed of our experience. Even if we can rarely hope to see and can never expect ourselves to reap this second harvest, the opportunity to sow what others will gather is ours. and none can deny it to us if we choose to take it.

Chapter 12

HOME HELPS

F E W when they are past 70 are wise to try to manage with no assistance in the home. The number of those who attain the age of 80, when all need some help with heavy work, is steadily increasing. A rising proportion of people are living through the late eighties into the nineties, by which time physical failings due to age are usually marked, so that most are largely if not wholly dependent on others. Yet it is desirable that all should live their own lives and be independent for as long as possible: this period will be greatly prolonged if there is a little friendly care, and if food is adequate and suitably nourishing.

The provision of a Home Help Service is a Local Authority responsibility, though not a legal obligation. Some authorities recognize its value and provide a real service of which the cost is less than might be expected. A Home Help is in fact a domestic help provided by the authority for the old, the sick, and the physically handicapped. In this chapter we are concerned with the help they can give to the old. In 1957 there were some 45,000 Home Helps, who gave assistance to over 250,000 families. But there are probably between 500,000 and 600,000 people aged over 70 living alone in this country, and about two thirds of that number are aged over 75; many have relatives, friends or neighbours to help them and some are sufficiently active to manage wholly for themselves, but when to these are added all the other folk who need assistance, as well as cases of sudden illness and the like, it would appear that there is room for a considerable increase if the hands can be found, with benefit to all.

The scheme started in 1942, when the then Minister of Health, Mr Ernest Brown, encouraged local authorities to provide Home Helps for lying-in mothers who, far from their relations, could find no one else to look after them. Later, Home Helps visited also the sick, feeble, and mentally deficient, as well as children needing attention. Today nearly all county councils and county boroughs provide Helps, though they are not so much in demand in country districts where there is more neighbourliness.

Where help is needed but the person concerned is unable to find it for one reason or another, the local authority can try to do so, and the individual will pay the whole or part of the cost; where it cannot be afforded, the local authority will pay. Curiously, some local authorities evade the provision of Home Helps, or supply them grudgingly, in order to keep down the rates; that thereby hospital beds are unnecessarily filled they profess is not their concern . . . thinking more in keeping with the old days of Public Assistance and Poor Law Hospitals than with modern times. None the less the idea is spreading, and it is significant that the annual cost of the Home Help service had risen from £2½ million in 1949-50 to £7½ million in 1957-8.

The great value of a Home Help is that someone will be coming in and out: someone will be doing the heavier work: someone will be helping to prepare the main meal most days and taking enough interest in it to see that it is adequate: someone will be bringing gossip and chatter into the four walls: someone will be keeping open a watchful eye, will detect little changes before they become big, and can seek and obtain such help as may be needed: someone will be helping to keep standards up and interests alive. This should be a matter of special concern to all of us.

The provision of a Home Help to an older person should not be too long delayed. In the earlier seventies an hour or two a week may suffice, yet be invaluable. Not only can the heavy work be done, but the idea of assistance will be more acceptable in the future when it is a real need, and as the years pass the hours of help can be gradually increased. It is quite wrong to delay until so late in life that a person has become feeble.

If the provision of help is delayed, standards will fall and the home become uncared for and untidy: later, dirty. Nutrition will be affected with a consequent loss of interest in and desire for food by a person otherwise still relatively independent. Then a Home Help may well not be acceptable to the aged person, and anyhow the conditions of work will be unduly difficult and unpleasant. The aim must always be to keep up standards, rather than to try to lift them once they have fallen. When people are old they have their own ways of life and are not likely to alter them; those who have sunk will most likely stay down.

In general, it is the single person who most needs a Home Help. Aged people who live alone comprise by far the largest proportion of the hard core of real problems, social and medical. An adequate Service, properly organized and properly applied, can relieve our social conscience of many most difficult cases by preventing them from developing. In all but a very few it could prevent the deterioration which is rarely seen when two or more old people are living together.

It is essential that any Home Help Service shall be properly organized, and its efficiency will depend on whether or not the right person is at the head. This usually means the appointment of a whole-time Home Help Organizer, with one or more assistants and the co-operation of the Health Visitors whose duties include the care of the aged and who do invaluable work but have many other calls on their time. Properly organized, it should only be in the exceptional case that it will not be possible to introduce a Home Help in the early stages before there is obvious need.

There is room for more Home Helps, and in most places the demand is greater than the supply. This is work which could appeal to many middle-aged or elderly people who are able to spare an hour or two or more a day (some Home Helps are on a half-time or whole-time basis and visit a number of people) and thus make a world of difference to the old and sick who are in need of assistance and understanding. There is a vast untapped source of Helps among people who would be willing but do not appreciate the opportunity open to them. So many elderly women struggle along on National Assistance who—after consulting the National Assistance Officer—could do five or six officials hours a week (in practice they would probably do much more for the love of it) and earn a little extra money without loss of benefit; they would be of an age to understand and give enough help to one who needs just a little to retain independence, and could themselves find a new and satisfying interest in life. The rates of pay are fixed on a national scale. For those on a whole-time basis, who visit maybe a number of people each day, travelling between places of work is paid for, there are holidays with pay, and uniform may be provided. Application either for a Home Help, or to become one, should be made to the Medical Officer of Health for the district.

It is a matter of experience that the best Home Helps are not seeking what they can get out, but what they can put in; their real reward is the happiness they are able to bring to people who cannot care for themselves, rather than the money. The number of solitary people who by reason of weakness or age or ill-health, and of those who can only be discharged from hospital if there is someone who can give some care at home, is increasing and is likely to increase. This could provide the future with a difficult social problem which should be prepared for and can be avoided if there is action now. As I wrote in an earlier chapter, it is best for the elderly to look after, be friendly with and help the old and if possible to be paid for it. This Service can provide the means to those who are able and willing to be neighbourly.

Chapter 13

DEPENDENCE AND LONELINESS

I

M o s t men marry and the majority early lose any desire for independence they may ever have had; which may be why the difficulties caused by independence in the later years usually affect the female sex. It is one of the most admirable traits of women that they will not give up, and this in spite of the known fact that when old they suffer from a proportionately greater number of physical disabilities than men. They pursue their daily round in spite of their limitations, and live longer because they keep themselves better interested and occupied than the men for whom they do so much.

Reasonable independence and the desire to do as much as possible for oneself is sensible; and it is now generally accepted that when we are growing old we should continue to live our own lives free from the too-close supervision of others however dear to us they may be. We need to be fully occupied, and this we cannot do if we are waited on. But quite early in retirement we begin to notice some physical limitations; indeed, if we are honest with ourselves we find out a number before we retire. Experience will teach us whilst we are still active (even if past our best) that it is tiring and often painful to struggle with tasks which have become too heavy for us; age in years is a bad yardstick because people vary so much.

The truth is that only the dead are independent of their fellows: some of us are or make ourselves be less dependent than others. This is only harmful when it becomes a matter of pride, for if pride governs our minds we struggle on when there is more to do than we can manage. I well remember one old friend who found increasing difficulty in getting in her coals from the shed: a bucket, then only half a bucket was heavy, there were two steps and the crazy paving was always irregular and sometimes slippery. Instead of getting in help for an hour a day, she stopped having coal fires, because 'she felt warm enough without', and the workings of her old mind naturally dictated that this should include electric fires; so she denied herself the warmth all old people need, and there can be no question that by so doing she hastened ill-health. This is the usual sequel to undue independence—that after a time we go without something we need, and in the long run this will hasten our complete dependence on others.

Moreover when we go without something we need, it affects not only our health but our standards. This causes us to be unhappy, and when we are unhappy we are usually less pleasant companions: so we are thrust more and more into our own company. Be independent by all means, but let it be with humility in your heart; there is nothing undignified in seeking assistance if ill-health or honourable years compel it. We need the help of others just as we need the company of others: the alternative to the one is often unendurable toil, and to the other is loneliness.

II

Some who reach the late sixties and early seventies (usually the more active and intelligent ones who have led full lives) have a distressing period when there is a subconscious realization that the world is quietly slipping away; and is leaving them increasingly remote spectators of the scene in the changes of which they may once have played an active part. It is a Phase of Struggle which is not recognized or understood either by them or by the rest of their world which detects (and often suffers from the consequence of) a difference in temper and outlook which for a time may make them difficult company. It arises in large part because they feel they are no longer needed, become painfully aware of their inadequacy, and think life is all behind.

If relatives and friends could understand that this springs from unhappiness of mind, and in some measure could appreciate how much is being suffered, they would often be more

96

tolerant. But sometimes it happens that such a person turns sour and bitter; nothing is right, no one is right, the world is not what it was, nor the people in it. Suspicions grow, past injustices rankle, the conversation leaves a feeling of distaste. It is akin to the distress of mind of the adolescent, which can prove such a trial to parents; and the remedy is the same, love and understanding, lots and lots of it. But the difficulty is that it is one thing for parents to give love and understanding to their offspring, and another for a younger generation or a contemporary to give it to one who seems determined to alienate all his friends. St Philip Neri wrote that excessive sadness has in general no other root than pride: things past redress should always be past care.

Given understanding, and patience, the phase will largely pass after a year or two and a kinder, softer outlook take its place. If there is some physical disability, such as blindness, a sense of grievance may remain and obtrude itself. With more general recognition of the condition, people of good will should not find it too difficult to help the sufferer over the trying years, however often they may be rebuffed.

Loneliness, anxiety, and lack or loss of interests—especially in those who in the past have lived full and active lives—may lead to neglect of personal care. For such an old one will know he will not be going outside the house, nor is anyone likely to come to see him; and so in time he comes to make ever-lessening attempts to maintain reasonable standards and his neglect of personal care is usually associated with neglect of the home. This is the simple sequence of events which can reduce to a pitiable state one who formerly had dignity and was a friend.

III

The complete dependence on others which comes to the infirm is usually accepted by them, though often only with heart burning for the loss of powers and regret for the trouble to others it causes. But in old age we more readily accept what is an act of God, and if we are becoming unable to care for ourselves we ought to look in this way on our increasing depend-

G   97

ence. 'To sit still, to be wholly dependent on other people, to be a burden and a more or less irksome strain on other people— it is then a heavy task, calling for courage and patience, to realize that independence is completely lost. One is thankful for help, and duly grateful for kindness, but complete resignation needs to be cultivated. Happiness now lies in memories of past joys, and in present heaven-sent sound mentality.' So wrote to me a lady of 94, a stranger, who until well past 80 was not only able to care for herself but active for others. 'I take comfort in the belief that if the Almighty keeps one alive when very old, He has purpose in so doing. There is certainly no "degradation" in the dependence of old age. I think the real crux is giving up one's independence gracefully, accepting as a fact that one is apparently of no use to one's friends, neighbours, and the people of the everyday world who would really have more time and energy for work of a profitable kind if you, the aged, were off the map. Most people want to be of *use* in life, and not necessarily out of vain-glory, but honestly as their natural aim and duty towards God and man.' So she continued.

I report to you some of her observations written so clearly in her own hand. She affirms that trust in a Good Providence which is so much in the minds of most old people, the fruit of the experience of a long life.

I went to see her. She was crippled with arthritis and could not move about without help. She only had the use of the thumb and first finger of each hand: with one hand she wrote, with the other she had to support her head whilst she wrote, for it tended to fall forward. Yet these disabilities did not daunt her. 'I wish,' she said, 'that you would write an article on tact.' You will find her definition of tact in the next chapter on Friendly Visiting. If that chapter is helpful to those who are *not* good at visiting others, they owe it not to me but to her; and her belief that there was a purpose in her continued existence will have been well-founded. I came away feeling stimulated and refreshed and I knew that whatever age or disabilities, life can always be fruitful if we will it to be.

I never saw her again, for she died soon afterwards, but her last letter to me was advice about the writing of this book—

she was herself the author of a notable biography. It may be that she felt her work was done at last and that she had passed on her torch: and my belief that this was so has been an added spur to me to take all possible pains with this book which is now in your hand.

Independence is something to treasure, not jealousy to guard. Even when it silently melts away we still have something to offer—if it is only a grateful word to those who help us, or a thought for another like ourselves.

IV

When I made a survey of over a hundred people who lived alone—many of them my patients—I found that loneliness was the biggest problem in each of the groups aged between 65 to 70, and 71 to 75; but that among the 51 people who were aged between 76 and 93 only one complained of loneliness as a severe affliction. In the report of the National Assistance Board for 1954 which recounts the result of an inquiry by the Officers of the Board into the circumstances of 85,000 people aged over 80 who lived alone, it is stated that 'the over-riding impression left on the visiting officers by this large group of people is that while a few of them are distressingly lonely . . . the over-whelmingly majority are comparatively healthy, independent, reasonably contented, and in frequent touch with relatives and neighbours . . . but not neglected and not unfriended.'

In general there are two principal kinds of loneliness in the early years of retirement. One is that caused by the loss of a lifetime partner with whom everything has been shared for many years and whose departure leaves an aching gap. The mutual dependence of two elderly people increases year by year, because one remains for the other the familiar landmark in life: each gives the other support and a sense of security. From this sort of loneliness only time can give some relief.

The second kind is often first noticed when isolation results from ill-health, or bad weather confines an independent person to the house for a long spell. Many enjoy living by themselves and—maybe—for themselves. But the price we may have to pay for independence can easily be excessive; all too often it is demanded when we are frail, and the friends in our diminishing circle are also failing in health. Maybe it is then, for the first time in our lives, that we are really thrown wholly on our own resources—to find them unexpectedly deficient. What we had previously counted to be an advantage has now gone sour. When we first find that we are not especially wanted, that nobody cares much, this indeed is loneliness. Though it is for contact with the younger generations that the elderly crave, in fact with contemporaries comes a fuller freedom, and there is no better happiness than this. The feeling of not being needed and of having no part in the lives of others is at the root of all loneliness, and is hard to bear.

To do something for somebody else gives a feeling of being wanted. No one need be dull and lonely if they can interest themselves in other people and do their best to help them. One elderly correspondent wrote that 'the lonely are those who are surrounded with work or small jobs waiting to be done, but don't see them or don't want to see them. To them time is long because they have never learned to fill it.' But though there is truth for some in what she writes, others have physical handicaps, others have not got over the shock of bereavement. Yet others of us are shy and timid and self-conscious by nature. But she does make the point that the cause of loneliness lies within ourselves, as must any possibility of cure. The truth is that unless we have enough contact with people so that we can do things for them, life will inevitably tend to get narrower and narrower and without self-sufficiency that is loneliness.

To keep fully occupied is the great secret of a relatively happy old age, for if we can fill our days, loneliness will not trouble us. But our kith and kin and friends and neighbours are the great standby, and we must encourage them: the supreme pleasure of advancing years is friendship. No one who in active life takes trouble to turn acquaintances into friends will be lonely in retirement. It is good to search out and to find someone worse off than ourselves, and to offer them some small service to help them in their loneliness or difficulty. If we obey an impulse to do a kindness we may at times be rebuffed, but at others the small act will meet with eager gratitude. It is good if we can be of some use, best of all when it is to our own folk; because our family and our friends are our contacts with the world.

In the later years there is much hidden loneliness: not only hidden but also accepted and not acutely felt. Younger people have their own business to attend to; their affairs and those of their children must of necessity preoccupy them. This trend always has been and always will be the way of the world; it is more noticeable at the present time, because the increase in the numbers of the old has been accompanied by full employment and the drift of many married women to well-paid whole-time work. The situation must mean that less attention can be paid to the older members of many families; some feel the deprivation acutely, but to others it gives an opportunity for usefulness which they hardly hoped would happen.

Because in the late sixties and early seventies we may find that the world in which we once were active is slipping away from us, we greatly value renewed contacts with it. Those who are not infirm, but have had a period of isolation in which they have sampled loneliness, have been given a warning they will be wise to heed. When health is restored and activity again becomes possible, they will do well if they can work out some way of lessening future distress. They cannot hope to escape it altogether, but by taking thought they may be able sensibly to diminish it. There are others in the same position, and there is always someone worse off.

Days which seemed endless in youth pass quickly in advanced old age. This is a blessing which helps along those who are housebound or bed-fast, though sometimes from hour to hour the minutes seem to drag and even the best-loved occupations to fail. Many learn, in the distress of the solitary hours, how to look into their own hearts. There they can find comfort, can rediscover the fact that they are not alone, nor are they forgotten. For God is with them as He is with all of us always.

Chapter 14

FRIENDLY VISITORS

L O N E L I N E S S—at all ages—is more frequent in towns than in villages; kindly people have given much thought to organizing ways in which it can be lessened. What is often forgotten is that many lonely people are by nature solitary in disposition. A lonely old person is often one who is infirm, or has always been inclined to be unsociable (though this may not at first sight be apparent) or is unhappy.

Early in retirement, when people are forming the pattern of the life they will follow now that active work has ceased, it is kind to include in the programme of things-to-be-done some thought for others who are lonely, solitary, or housebound. Friendliness and neighbourliness should be the motives which inspire. There is a world of difference between 'Visiting' and 'Friendly Visiting': the heart must be full and warm as well as the head and, occasionally, the hands. Some people can be very lonely in the midst of their family, as well as in Homes for old people and in hospitals.

Not everyone is by nature gifted to be a friendly visitor. If the quality is not yours it is as well to recognize it, because though it can be cultivated with some degree of success in those to whom it does not come naturally, it is difficult to alter one's disposition.

The essentials for successful friendly visiting are enough time, mutual liking, and a sufficient degree of common interests and understanding and tact. By tact is meant the ability to put oneself in another's place and understand their feelings, to try to see what we say and do when we are visiting old Mrs Jones through old Mrs Jones' eyes. It is because these conditions are more often filled by contemporaries, and by the elderly, that they are usually more satisfying as friendly visitors to the old and aged than the younger generation. It is important, too, that a friendly visitor should have a professional person, like a health visitor or district nurse or doctor, to whom to turn if in need of help or advice.

The old like to have the young about them, none the less; but in the hearts of many is a feeling that in fact the latter have little liking for or interest in them. This is only half true, and therefore misleads. Old people day-dream a good deal, and spend much time looking back along the long road they have come; for many, perhaps most, these things and the progress of the following generations are now their principal concern. The elderly also like to remember time past, and have this in common with the old; but they still have active interests to occupy them, and their horizons are not so near. The young, on the other hand, are devoting themselves to the difficulties of the present and of the unknown future, to their children and to other pursuits; however dutiful they may be and however deep their affection, they cannot have a great deal of time or thought to spare for the generation which long ago walked along the path which they now wish to explore for themselves.

In some fortunate places there is a Friendly Visiting Service. The kind people who serve in it often go far beyond simple neighbourliness, for besides visiting and being sociable they may help with shopping or housework, take an infirm person to church or chapel, even prepare meals. They would be better called Friends-in-Need, for they do incalculable good; their charity is not the cold rather patronizing type which is resented and often feared, but that practical Christianity which warms the heart because the goodwill which inspires it can be felt.

There is one warning. Let your help be fairly regular, but not absolutely by rule. Old people—yourself in a few years—are mostly rather self-centred, especially those who are lonely, and will be disappointed if you do not appear when you are expected. A small personal gift—a pot of home-made jam, some flowers from the garden, a magazine—will be appreciated. But for the same reason do not always take a gift or it will be apt to be taken for granted that you will do so: then any failure to bring one for whatever reason will be either resented or may cause anxiety lest offence has been given. If your visits and gifts are at your convenience and not by rule they will always be welcomed by a lonely person with time to spare, and you your-self will not feel tied too much: for what becomes an obligation will some time be a nuisance.

There is always someone who will be glad of your company if you are prepared to be neighbourly, and the older we get the less social distinctions seem to matter. Some people who are solitary by temperament may seem not to want to be visited, but very few will fail to be greatly helped by kindly, friendly, tactful interest. It is not wise to take on too much, but if you can find two or three or perhaps four who need you (if possible include one who is 'difficult' in one way or another) and if your personality will fit in with theirs, be sure of this . . . you will give much happiness by taking the trouble to be a friend in deed.

II

During the last few years several firms, usually moved by a forward thinking Pensions, Personnel or Welfare Officer, have started Welfare schemes for their former employees, whose number, in proportion to those on the active list, and in the absence of major changes, will be about 1 to 10. The principal function of many of these is to organize Friendly Visiting by selected pensioners who volunteer to see other ex-employees. The value of a scheme which also maintains links with a man's working past and may keep him in touch with his former fel-lows is easy to see. The usefulness and helpfulness, which the Visitor must feel, will add special satisfactions to his own retire-ment as well as maintaining some active links with the firm.

A Visitor is chosen from the younger pensioners, and selec-tion is helped by knowledge from his working days of his out-look and qualities. Each is responsible for visiting about twelve or more pensioners who either live near his home or—better—whose background is similar to his own. From time to time Visitors will meet together for discussion, perhaps with the director of the scheme: this not only stimulates but guides them.

The first visits are usually preceded by a card, the ice may need thawing: often the Visitor will take his wife with him, especially if the pensioner to be visited is a woman. In general, the aim is that every pensioner shall be visited at least once or twice a year. On special occasions such as 80th and subsequent birthdays, or golden and diamond wedding anniversaries, there will usually be either a visit, or some other reminder of the firm's interest through its Welfare scheme. Where a pensioner seems cut off or lives alone or there is other need or difficulty, the Visitor will call much more frequently than where it may seem hardly necessary. Sometimes, especially on birthdays and at Christmas, when it is quite a natural thing to do, a small gift will be taken or it may be sent by the firm, whichever seems more suitable. These schemes vary in the details of what they do, but the principles are basically the same: but flexibility, even between what is done by one Visitor and another, within limits is to be encouraged.

Visitors should come from all levels, but none can afford to be out of pocket. They must be able to claim expenses and the cost of gifts if these are purchased—some schemes supply gifts from stocks—and these claims should quickly be met by the Welfare scheme. The claim form can also be a record of visits and comments which can be studied by the director of the scheme. One aim should be to reduce to a minimum writing and such like by Visitors.

Naturally a scheme is easier to organize by a large firm than by a small one and for most of the latter, unless purely local, it will be impracticable: even the large firms can only keep in touch with a portion of former employees. But any scheme to succeed must have the right kind of mind somewhere at the back of it.

One of the pioneers was the Unilever Pensions Welfare Organization, and a study of its work after seven years by the London Pensions Manager, Mr P. I. Clemow, in the summer number 1963 of the House Magazine closes with these words:— 'The Organization arose as a means of alleviating loneliness among a portion of the Company's pensioners. It has grown into something more. It is a link between many who knew one another when at work and had lost touch. It is a link between the pensioners and the Company in which they worked, in many cases a long time ago. It provides a social service which has been of great value to individual pensioners who have fallen on hard times or run into difficulties not of their own making. It is a living demonstration of the value of a timeless asset—the human touch'.

Chapter 15

WISE WAYS WITH EYES

O N E day when I was small I pointed out to my grandmother a battleship riding in a bay a mile away: and it deeply impressed me when she said her eyes were not strong enough for her to see it. She was not blind, but she was old, and she did not have suitable glasses. So she missed seeing this, and much more. Only one person in twenty reaches the age of retirement without finding a need for glasses, either for reading, for long distance vision, or both.

The reason for this is simple: the changes due to time. You will help your eyes as much as possible by having a good but not glaring light when you are reading or sewing, by not over-tiring them with too much fine work at once, and by ensuring that you have a suitable diet. But apart from these things there is not much else to be done, beyond preserving your general health and avoiding excess of anything.

If you need glasses, be wise and obtain them: for you will miss so much. Go to your doctor and ask him for a certificate for sight-testing, or if you find it difficult to get to your doctor, ask him to call to see you. He is your best friend in such matters. If he agrees, go to an ophthalmic medical practitioner or optician: under the National Health Service examination by either is free. It is so important to detect disease of the eye in the early stages that many doctors advise their elderly patients to see an ophthalmic medical practitioner: this is because although many opticians are first-class, and the standard is rising, quite a number lack the special training which will enable them to detect abnormalities of a medical nature which common sense tells us must become more common as age increases. An ophthalmic medical practitioner can prescribe glasses for you, but he cannot dispense them. After seeing him you can take his prescription to any optician you choose and obtain them at the National Health Service rates. Take care not to allow yourself to be persuaded to pay a fancy price for a frame by an over business-like optician, for those provided under the N.H.S. are excellent —or should be: if in doubt consult your doctor.

If your glasses are going to suit, you will know within a few days of having them. If they do not, you must within a week or two go back to the ophthalmic medical practitioner or optician. It may be that your eyes were tired the day they were tested, or you were not very well. If an optician tested your eyes he will retest, and if he still cannot suit, he must send you back to your doctor. The latter will probably ask for a specialist's opinion because it may be that there is some disease of the eye or body, and not just ordinary wear and tear. So you see that if your glasses do not suit you must not let the matter slide: you may be neglecting to have some disease like diabetes dealt with when it is still easy to check it, whilst if there is no disease you are not obtaining the correct glasses you need in order to get as much as possible out of life. If they do not suit to begin with they are not likely to do so later, and may even do harm, so be very careful to ensure that you start right.

When, in 1954, I did a survey in a group of Oxfordshire villages of 107 people aged between 65 and 94 who lived alone, I found that at least 19 were in need of eye-testing. Of these 19 no less than 11 were physically unable to go to have this done because of the difficulties of travelling. If you ought to have your eyes tested and are so handicapped for whatever reason that you cannot go to get it done, ask your doctor if he can help you. It must be a great affliction to be in need of glasses, to be largely housebound, and possibly unnecessarily be unable to read or sew: worse still if you live alone. So why suffer? It is possible though not always easy for him to arrange either for you to have your eyes tested in your own home or to be taken to a hospital where it can be done. The National Health Service provides that examination of the eyes in the patient's own home can be effected either by an ophthalmic medical practitioner or an optician, and this is a regular feature of their work. They have portable equipment which they carry to the patient's home, even to the bedside if necessary, and carry out the examination to determinate the condition of the eyes and prescribe the best correction. Opticians receive no extra payment for this service but none the less provide it if requested.

Failing eyesight is usually a slow process if it is due only to the changes of time. When it is brought about by disease it is often more rapid, and it will not be corrected by glasses for long if at all. Be careful not to pretend to yourself that all is well when it is not, nor pride yourself on not having to wear glasses or you may forego obtaining them when you need them. If you will be careful to be honest with yourself all will be well. Even well-suiting glasses will need changing after a few years, and it is worthwhile to have this done. Pain in the eye, seeing haloes around lights, or attacks of foggy vision however slight, are a reason for seeking medical advice immediately; one or other often seems to come on after a visit to a cinema or watching television in a darkened room. Once damage has occurred it is difficult to diminish, much less to cure, so early treatment is important.

Dr Sheldon, in his Wolverhampton survey in 1946, found that about one third of the elderly and old people seen had unsuitable glasses; some of these were inefficient, some of them harmful. Since then the National Health Service should materially have reduced the proportion because expense was a major factor at that time. In addition, the help given by the National Assistance Board makes it easy for those in receipt of benefit to obtain glasses.

Quite a number of people use glasses which have been given to them or which they have inherited and taken to. Dr Sheldon found that two thirds of these were unsuitable, and a considerable number were definitely harmful. It may not be good business to look a gift horse in the mouth, but it seems a wise policy when the horse takes the form of spectacles.

To sum up, then, you are almost certain to need glasses at least for reading when you get older; be wise, have the need filled. You should not merely have your eyes properly tested but in your best interests ensure that the glasses are suitable when you get them: going back to the ophthalmic medical practitioner or optician within a week or two if they are not, as a protection against early disease of the eye. You should have your eyes retested when necessary, regularly if possible and can be pretty sure to need to do so within five years. It will be in your best interests never to use glasses which have belonged to someone else because there is a good chance that they may do harm.

II

Vision, when it begins to fail, can be much helped by good light. Especially is the vision of the elderly less effective after dark. Ill-lit, twisting staircases are particular danger spots for the old, but any dark corner in a house or flat is a potential menace. Fireplaces, cookers and sinks encourage bending forwards if the lighting is bad, and old people may easily overbalance and fall. The difficulties of old folk if outdoors in the dark are often forgotten by younger members of old people's clubs and the like, and meetings and parties are best held in daylight.

One of the peculiarities of the changing vision in the elderly is a diminished power to adapt to sudden changes in intensity of light. They may be able to see quite well in a room that they know, even when the lighting is not satisfactory: but may find extreme difficulty on leaving a room, walking outside at night or climbing stairs which are not well lit. Great care therefore must always be taken not to hurry when going from a light into a dark room or passage. Because of this slow adaption to sudden change elderly people are unwise to drive motor cars at night unless they are quite sure they can recover vision reasonably quickly after meeting on-coming headlights. Nor should the likelihood of the difficulty caused by a wet or dirty windscreen be overlooked, and unnecessary risks will be avoided by the simple expedient of accepting the position and allowing some-one else to drive.

III

And if the light goes? The loss of any faculty is hard to bear. But it will happen to some, who must be prepared to accept what they cannot alter. It is human nature for the sighted to feel for and want to help the blind. But so many try to conceal their failing vision, resent offers of assistance, try to go their own way, and merely complicate life for others. When a blind person refuses to use a white stick, it is hard on people who are unaware of his disability but have to allow for it: yet, as one old friend said to me, 'If I wave my white stick every policeman in London comes to help me.' If your vision fails, don't be too proud to seek help, but don't attempt to seek pity or sympathy: blind people should forget the words 'I wish. . . .' because they tend to sour the milk of human kindness which is theirs unsought.

I V

Cataract operations still are dreaded by many. With improved skills the quacks who thrive on the fearful are gradually going out of business. It is tedious to have to wait. It is even more tedious to have one eye operated on and one eye not—rather like having one long leg and one shorter. No one likes a prospect of surgery but the chances of success are great. If you have a cataract have courage. All is *not* lost.

Chapter 16

HARD OF HEARING

A B O U T one person in eight between 65 and 75 is severely or moderately deaf: of those aged over 75, a quarter or more are similarly affected. Comparatively few people consult a doctor about their disability until it is severe or total; such delay is unfortunate, for by then it is much more difficult to give the help which is available. It is as well to be quite sure that deafness is not caused by wax; but in most cases it is due to the delicate hearing apparatus losing its sensitivity, and because of this, the slow progress with advancing years can neither be prevented nor cured.

Hearing depends so much on the amount of attention paid to what is being said, that there may appear to be a great deal of truth in the common belief that a deaf person is only as deaf as he chooses to be. It is an unfair criticism, for all people tend to hear the sounds they want to hear and exclude the others from consciousness. For example, if we sit absorbed in a book or television programme, we are usually quite cut off from the sounds which are all around us—even those made by burglars —unless for one reason or another something disturbs our concentration.

When hearing begins to fail, sounds are specially liable to go unnoticed, because they have to struggle through the barrier of lessened sensitivity in the ear or nerve of hearing before they reach the mind, which then may only perceive the weakened sensations if it is on the alert for them. When for some reason their attention strays from the traffic, for example, the hard-of-hearing are especially liable to be involved in street accidents: though much the same thing can happen to anyone—like an absent-minded professor—who has some problem on his mind which is engaging all his thoughts. Conversely, blind people are rarely deaf because listening has their whole attention.

Impaired hearing is usually first noticed when one is being

112

spoken to in a crowded or noisy place. It is then found that listening is easiest when one person is talking in a quiet room as clearly as possible about something which interests. Curiously, shouting does not help so much as might be expected: not only does it tend to worry a deaf person, but the clearness of the words is diminished, and the help most deaf people gain by watching the lips of the speaker is also lost: many deaf people unconsciously watch the lips of those who are speaking to them. Those who lose their hearing slowly can become very good at lip-reading, and in this way can help out what remains of the failing sense: it can be practised in front of the television by turning down the sound. Impaired vision and blindness bring with them sympathy and help; deafness tends to cause irritation when it is necessary to shout or repeat. Patience and kindness are much appreciated by the hard-of-hearing.

Hearing aids are of most value when increased loudness is necessary to overcome loss of sound; they do not clarify sounds but make them louder. A hearing aid is like a magnifying glass only; the need for clear speech still remains. Because being hard-of-hearing is a slowly progressive condition, it is sensible at a very early stage to take to a hearing aid and to become used to it. This will not give perfect hearing, but it will enable a persevering user to 'get by' for many years, and will save friends from much discomfort. The need for early use of a hearing aid arises from the fact that, ordinarily, we hear only the sounds we want to, or have forced on our attention; we learned in childhood to ignore the mass of background noises—like the chirping of birds or the traffic outside the window—which none the less are there. Indeed, some townpeople cannot sleep when they stay in the country because the night is so quiet and still, and they miss all the background noises to which ordinarily they pay no attention.

If people have allowed themselves to become so deaf that they get out of the life-long habit of 'listening', they have to learn afresh to disregard these background noises which are magnified by the aid just as much as the sounds they crave to hear. The process of relearning may take months of careful application; the older they are, the less likely will they be to bother, though if this easy course is followed they themselves will be the greatest losers in the long run. But if early in deafness the condition and its slowly progressive nature are recognized, a very great deal can be done to keep going a sense no one can afford to lose. If it were possible to have a hearing rehabilitation service recognized as a need for the elderly, this difficulty could to a large extent be overcome. There are a few centres for this purpose, as at Oxford; but with these exceptions there seem to be neither the money nor the trained personnel with time to spare. So for most the remedy is to commence to use a hearing aid as soon as minor difficulties are noticed.

The old Health Service general issue hearing aid is efficient, but has to be bulky because it must be robust. The original N.H.S. hearing aid with separate batteries is gradually being replaced by a N.H.S. transistor model. Commercial hearing aids though expensive—£60 is quite a usual charge—are not more efficient but often much handier, and are more delicate: the manufacturers' guarantee usually only lasts for one year and does not cover damage by dropping it. Before purchasing a hearing aid always ask someone qualified—and preferably impartial —to give an opinion if it is likely to give you good service, and insist on having it on approval to try it out before it is paid for. It is essential that a hearing aid should be in perfect working order, and ensuring this perfection is worth any time and trouble which may be necessary.

Since reading is a great comfort to those who are hard-of-hearing, it is especially important that glasses, if needed, should be satisfactory. The wireless is useful when practising the use of a hearing aid; but unless you live alone, never turn it up too loud. Television is an even greater help to deaf people; it provides features in which it is not necessary to hear the words, but there are many more in which it is possible to see the speaker talking, and to hear the better because he is speaking quietly and clearly about something in which one is interested. There will be programmes which will be of no use at all; but in general it can be a great new interest to those shut off from the world by the barrier of deafness.

Instruction in lip-reading can be a great help to the deaf, and there are trained experienced teachers in some hospitals. Even a little accomplishment in lip-reading can bring considerable gain of the sense of communication.

There is little wisdom in attempting to conceal deafness. It is better to be frank about the disability—for it is only a handicap and not a stigma. A hearing-aid should be as much taken for granted as spectacles or false teeth: and when all is said deafness is common at all ages. But in general people will speak up if the disability is known. There was a salesman who advertised a 'hearing-aid' which he sold in a sealed envelope for half-a-crown: this was found to be a button on a piece of plastic-covered wire, with instructions to put the button in the ear, and the other end of the plastic inside the breast pocket—and people would talk more loudly when they saw it.

When speaking to a deaf person it is best to rivet their attention by putting a hand on their chair or arm or knee, or by saying their name first 'Mrs Brown (or Granny or Uncle Joe) isn't it a lovely day' rather than 'Isn't it a lovely day, Mrs Brown.' This so often saves the wearisome business of repeating some trivial remark.

To avoid having the volume of the radio on uncomfortably high, it is possible to have a small extension loud-speaker plugged into a set, with a very long flex, and speaker (about 8 in. sq.) can then stand on a shelf or table by the better ear of the deaf person—and then everyone can listen in comfort.

Chapter 17

PAINFUL FEET

I

A F E W years ago I was talking to an old farmer friend whose feet almost crippled him, and urged him to go to get his corns cut because it would make such a difference to him. On a later visit I noticed that he was getting about freely, and remarked that I was pleased he had taken my advice and was so much more comfortable. 'Yes,' he said, 'my feet are much easier but I didn't get my corns out: I've taken to Wellingtons. If I don't wear them for too long or get my feet cold, and if I keep changing my socks, I find them much kinder than those old boots, and my corns don't hurt at all except when it is going to rain.'

Just about that time I had been hearing so much about the need for chiropody services, and the crippling many old people were said to suffer, that I decided to do a small survey in my own practice. I saw 120 people aged between 60 and 85 to find out some plain facts, and how they dealt with their difficulties. The only patient whom I knew to be housefast because of foot troubles was afflicted with severe chilblains—and then, of course, only in winter.

Half these 120 patients had no discomfort from their feet at all; and the difficulties due to corns on the toes and callouses on the soles seemed to diminish as age increased and individuals became less active. This was important, because it is often said that such disorders are a *frequent* cause of housefastness in the aged. The greatest disability I found to be caused not by corns or callouses, but by horny toenails and in a few by bunions which caused much pain. The most comfortable of those who had corns and callouses were those who were able to deal with their feet in their own homes regularly once a week. Those who went to a chiropodist—almost exclusively those who lived on a bus route—seemed apt to have a week of bliss, a fortnight of growing discomfort, and a week of pain before the next monthly visit was due. There were some few who for one reason or another were unable to obtain any care for their troubles, and who suffered a good deal in consequence, but they seemed to get out and about in spite of it; they were mostly those who could not stoop to get at their feet, and had no relative or neighbour to help them out. Villages are friendly helpful places, and the good neighbour is common: so it is likely that there is a great proportion of these unfortunates in the towns.

I I

If between the time people begin to stagger at about one year until they reach the age of 70, they are on their feet for only twenty minutes a day, they will walk a distance equal to the circumference of the earth at its equator—25,000 miles. It has been estimated that in fact most people use their feet to the equivalent of walking nearer a quarter of a million miles during their lifetime. Yet foot troubles in old age after so many years of use, however painful, are mostly only minor ones, the vast majority of them in women.

During middle age feet may compel themselves increasingly to be noticed. In common with the rest of the body, they tend to get larger: but especially in women they are usually crammed into the same size of shoes as before—and very unsightly the result may look. If well-proportioned, a larger shoe on such a woman can look more elegant as well as being much more comfortable, and the lower heel which is in keeping is another step in the right direction. It is a mistake to change suddenly from high heels to wearing low ones: it is a great advantage to be able to wear either, and to do so. Women as they get older should try to give more thought to comfort, for any slight resultant loss of elegance is compensated in other ways; if a mature woman is charming and attractive a man is going to pay less attention to her feet and ankles than he will to those of a younger woman who lacks the poise of maturity.

Foot Strain

Because of the lessened resilience of the feet—in common with that of the rest of the body—which arises during and after middle age, and which will of course be aggravated by any substantial increase in weight, it is important to avoid foot strain. The commonest cause of this is standing still, because then the circulation to the feet is diminished. To be able to stand for long periods without ill-effect there must first have been sufficient exercise and sufficient rest: in town life most people get practically no exercise and far too much standing, which makes the circulation sluggish and the muscles fatigue easily. Most elderly people are quite unable to stand still for more than a few minutes; the feet are not to blame but the conditions which are imposed on them. Another cause of foot-strain is *sudden* change from a sedentary occupation to an active or—worse—a standing one: the foot and its muscles must have time to adapt themselves especially during and after middle age. It is essential, moreover, to have footwear which gives real support to the feet if they are not to collapse altogether after a change of this kind. Immediately after an illness bedroom slippers and warm socks are wise; but early in convalescence, because of the effect of debility on the muscles, bedroom slippers should be discarded in favour of shoes which give support.

Corns on the Toes

These are caused by the pressure of boots or shoes. Some elderly men habitually wear hard heavy boots: light ones are more comfortable, especially in retirement, and they are no better for being tight. Easy footwear—not loose—will relieve pressure on a painful corn: the first step to curing it.

If there is a corn and permanent comfort is sought (and provided there is no severe deformity of the toes or feet) it is desirable to have two pairs of shoes which do not press on the corn.

Corns are rarely cured just by cutting away the hard skin. At the same time it is necessary to remove this skin, once suitable shoes have been obtained, because then they should be even more comfortable and all pressure is to be avoided. This can be done by paring the corn—the safest way is with a corn plane such as most chemists can supply or will obtain—or scraping it after soaking, or getting a chiropodist to deal with it. Unless the corn is very hard it is usually effective to put on one of the collodian corn plasters for forty-eight hours. After removal apply a pad of wet cotton wool overnight and cover with waterproof plastic or oilskin to keep in the moisture; the corn will usually be quite soft the next morning and some can be picked out. This should be done weekly until the corn is cured.

Cure of a corn is not so easy where there is deformity of the toes. The advice of a properly trained and qualified chiropodist should be sought. He will guide you about suitable footwear, or fashion a small appliance which will give relief by evening out any pressure.

Callouses

These occur on the sole in the region of the ball of the foot. They are not common in men except in waiters. They are very common in women because their high-heeled shoes throw the weight of the body forwards off the heels (where it should be), and also cramp the toes which normally also take some of the weight. The resultant pressure causes thickened layers of skin to form which press on the sensitive deeper tissues and cause pain and disability when stood on.

Those who suffer from callouses often—not always—become more comfortable as age advances, because the habits change. Heels tend to get lower, shoes wider, the feet are used less. Comfortable footwear is, again, the first essential to relief, and it is especially important that the toes shall not be cramped so that they, and the heel, can take some of the weight off the ball of the foot. But, I repeat, a sudden change from a high to a low heel is inadvisable: it must be done gradually. A rubber sole to the shoe is often helpful.

The pain is caused by a ridge of thick hard skin: in the first instance this may be pared or scraped away, or—better—softened with a collodion corn plaster as for a corn. After this it is desirable to give the foot a good soaking once a week: and the skin can be planed or scraped, or rubbed away with pumice;

with this regular system, feet can usually be kept very comfortable. A chiropodist may cut away the hard skin causing the callous, or he may pad the feet to distribute the pressure: but neither measure will effect a cure.

Most corn plasters and ointments contain salicylic acid, and this is excellent for softening a corn or callous. But on elderly feet it must be used with care, and not at all on those of sufferers from diabetes or bad circulation. Twenty-four or at most forty-eight hours at a time is long enough to leave it on: by the end of that time the skin will be softened and much can be removed. Another plaster or some more ointment should not be applied for four or five days or harm may be done. By the end of that time the tissues will have recovered, and it should be safe to give another treatment.

Injuries to the toes and feet in the old—such as may occur when corns and callouses are too closely or clumsily cut—may be dangerous: especially in those who suffer from diseases in which the blood supply tends to be poor, for this allows infection to get a hold and may lead to troublesome complications. That is why corn-cutting—no matter who does it—is not without risk. A competent chiropodist will give you good advice on the care of your feet, on your shoes, and kindred subjects. Anyone can cut corns and nails and pad feet, and some very queer people call themselves chiropodists and do these things (some of them very well): but only a fully trained and qualified chiropodist can give you the best treatment and advice.

Deformed Toe-nails are more common, and more crippling, than is generally realized. The nail is often grossly hardened, thickened and horn-like, and it is always very difficult to deal with it by ordinary means. The wearing of a shoe may be impossible, with consequent limitation of getting out and about (as on a wet day). Only a competent chiropodist is likely to have the apparatus and experience essential to deal with this truly formidable problem. Fortunately growth is slow, so that a visit once or twice a year will be all that is required to preserve a reasonable degree of comfort.

Bent Big Toe (Hallux Valgus) and Bunions

This is probably the most painful and most crippling of all the acquired deformities of the foot. It practically always occurs in women, and it is often associated with callosities (callouses) on the ball of the foot due to the same cause. A bunion is a painful and maybe inflamed swelling on the inner side of the head of the bone of the great toe at the broadest part of the foot: the great toe itself is twisted outwards, and by pushing the other toes so far as it can it often finishes up by over-riding them. Quite apart from the pain of the bunion, the pain of the callouses, and the painful arthritis which is liable to occur at the head of the great toe, the difficulties with footwear can be imagined.

This is a miserable and disabling complaint. Special footwear will help, for it must always be remembered that the cheap high-heeled shoe is a perfect means of producing the deformity. If suitable shoes are worn early, much relief can be obtained from supports designed to relieve excessive strain, or appliances which hold the toe in a better position or relieve pressure over the bunion. Regular visits may be paid to a competent chiropodist, both for the provision of specially made protective appliances, and advice and supervision with regard to footwear. The majority of affected feet can thus be kept reasonably free from pain almost indefinitely in spite of a considerable degree of deformity: the only alternative is operation which may be justified and in skilled hands with suitable after-care can be very successful in selected cases.

Chapter 18

THOUGHTS ON FOOD

I

C A R E F U L thought should be given early in retirement to food and drink, though one should not be too fussy or faddy, but enjoy eating if possible. Few when elderly or old are so placed for money that they can indulge themselves very much even if they wish to do so. For many it is a matter of living on the border-line; but it is important to keep on the right side of that line, not only in terms of money but also of the value of food to the body. To do this will make all the difference between good health and activity on the one hand and a disinclination to find interest in and to get much out of life on the other.

Most look upon eating as one of the pleasures of life, if a routine one. It is not easy to accustom oneself to the fact that proper food is essential to continued bodily well being. As people become older appetites tend to grow less keen, and the preparing and cooking of a meal more and more seems a time-wasting nuisance. Many say that they are doing less work and so do not need much food and that is true. But if they persist in this way it is very easy indeed for them to have less than they should. They do not feel ill; but they could feel a great deal better, though they may not realize it.

Often to a naturally lessening desire for food is added the cost of buying it and the trouble involved in shopping and cooking. So some tend, humanly, to take the easy way. The margin of safety of people who live alone without help is nearly always very low.

It must not be thought that it is desired to suggest a diet. Likes and reasonable dislikes must have their place; what is to be avoided is a wrong balance in what is eaten, due sometimes to a lack of knowledge, sometimes to cost, sometimes to the tendency to eat less, often to all these reasons.

There is a saying in law that ignorance is no defence. So it is with Nature. Those who are ignorant of her rules or ignore them, will have to pay for doing so. What makes things more difficult is that the more people get into wrong ways of eating and drinking the harder it becomes to make the effort to get out of those ways.

The essential needs of the body are not many. Fuel to burn up and to provide the heat and energy necessary to enable us to move about: mineral salts, like table salt, iron, bicarbonate of soda or calcium: the vitamins present in tiny quantities in certain foodstuffs: more fluid than most take. Because of the change and repair which are constantly going on, it needs material for replacement purposes. For example, it is believed that each red cell in the blood lives about a hundred days: there are probably more of these red cells floating round in the blood of any one of us than there have been human beings on this earth during the last quarter of a million years. Yet when each cell dies it has to be replaced, and though most of the material is used again there is always a little waste which must be made good. Our bodies are composed of millions of millions of cells of one kind or another.

As a rule unless the diet is deficient in quantity as well as in quality there are enough of the energy-giving substances and minerals present in the food. People tend to go short of those needed for repair and of the vitamins because these occur in the more expensive items. Fat we most dislike and do not greatly need.

Proper food will help to keep up activity and prevent ageing. Activity will assist the appetite and digestion because it stimulates the circulation and promotes an increased sense of well-being and the elimination of waste products. Moreover bones which are used are the stronger for it. A short walk after the midday meal will help digestion more than resting; it has been remarked with some truth that we should make our dinner go down to our feet.

11

The importance of proper food in lessening the weakness and failings usually ascribed to advancing years is only now becoming recognized. This is because the changes occur very gradually, because the subject is ill-understood, and because of the difficulty in finding out just what people do eat.

Moderation and regularity are two ideals at which to aim when we reach the middle and later years. We can be immoderate when we have too little of anything as well as when we have too much.

If too little food is taken (judged by quantity) the normally slow process of ageing is quickened. Soon there is increasing loss of appetite and of activity. followed slowly by apathy and depression. These will be aggravated if there is inadequate warmth. All of them cause disinclination to go out to obtain food, to prepare and cook it. So physical weakness becomes marked, and not a few in the advanced stage spend much or most of their time sitting in a chair or lying in bed; more and more in that event will they tend to 'let themselves go'.

The quantity of food can be adequate, but there may still be a deficiency in quality. There may be too little of those items (red meat, fish, cheese, eggs, we should have some of one or other at least every day) which help to keep the body in good working order and repair: or of necessary minerals and vitamins found in milk, vegetables, fruit, brown bread and liver. Although the onset is usually slower in this sort of wrong feeding, physical weakness becomes evident and again it is found that obtaining and preparing become more and more burdens which are evaded; especially by those who live—and cook—and eat—alone.

One good reason why it is believed that in a large number of aged people the simple weakness of body or mind which has been blamed on increasing years is in fact really due to food insufficient in quantity or in quality, is that when the fault has been corrected there can be a wonderful change for the better in health and strength, and a corresponding increase in happiness. This is why so many improve during a stay in hospital or on entering a Home. It is noticeable also when they have been living alone, have been failing, and have a relative to come to look after them: they often seem to take out a new lease on life.

It is a mistake to buy the cheapest food. Price must be looked to, of course, and a substantial proportion of what is purchased will be the inexpensive things. But some money must be set aside for the buying of certain necessary even if dear items. Some people get into their heads that they cannot afford food; this idea, and difficulties in shopping, are responsible for much avoidable ill-health and weakness. To go short of food or warmth are the greatest mistakes the elderly and old can make. It is a plain scientific fact that we each need wisely to spend at least 25s a week on food if we are to maintain health at the best level possible.

III

Milk is very near to being a perfect food; few people cannot take and enjoy it in one form or another. It is most nourishing when cold or warm; boiling and cooking destroy some of the vitamins, but do not otherwise affect its value as a food. It contains not only vitamins, and a balanced proportion of all the three principal foodstuffs, but also mineral salts such as the lime which keeps bones strong. To have a pint or more of milk a day is a sound foundation: it will help one to feel better, to resist minor illnesses, and to be protected against night cramps. This is an excellent habit, and one cannot get into it too soon. Dried and tinned milk are better than no milk; but natural food is best, and there is nothing like milk taken regularly. It is the most complete and easily digested food any person at any age can have and, for what it is, one of the cheapest. Not everyone likes it as a drink, though most can learn to do if they try. Those who do not like milk can usually take it in puddings, junkets, or blancmange, as well as mixed with malted milk, cocoa or coffee. Complan (Glaxo) is easily prepared and may be flavoured or sweetened.

Elderly vegetarians should give special thought to their diet, for money is probably a bigger factor than ever before. Instead of red meat, fish, liver and (possibly) eggs they will have to have extra milk, cheese, and peas and beans; and these frequently. They are especially liable to develop anaemia, so that green vegetables will be most important.

Fresh, dried or tinned peas and beans are cheap and a fair substitute for meat or fish: also valuable are cheap cereal foods such as rice, barley, oatmeal and cornflour. A good broth made with meat and bone stock, flavoured with root vegetables and containing potatoes and a sprinkling of peas, rice and barley, will be a highly palatable and nutritious midday dinner in winter time, especially with a dumpling cooked in it or with bread. As it will be quickly digested, it should be followed by bread and cheese.

Cheese is a most valuable food, and comparatively cheap. The ordinary kinds are much to be preferred to the processed if only because so much variety is available; but they keep less well, going either mouldy or dry, which is a great disadvantage to those who live alone. Buying anything in small enough quantities is one of the great difficulties: a joint however small, even a cabbage or a cauliflower, may all outstay their welcome; a small loin chop, or a little minced beef should always be tender and should have little waste as well as being tasty and easy to cook.

The time to be fitted with dentures is the fifties and early sixties, for few people will take to them in later life. Food properly chewed helps digestion, though the stomach is a very long suffering organ. So long as there are enough opposing natural teeth left for chewing they should usually be left in the jaws in people of 70 or more: for they will be more effective than false ones carried in the pocket, and there is little pleasure in eating mushy food, though the toothless jaws of some people have surprising powers to chew.

There are those who cannot or will not eat brown bread. Instead, one or two tablespoonfuls daily of Bemax or Froment (grocer or chemist) and white bread will do nearly as well. If there are difficulties about fruit and vegetables, or if fresh milk cannot be taken, one vitamin capsule (Caps. Vitaminorum B.P.C.) taken twice daily will be of great value; but there are other things in fruit and vegetables and milk than vitamins. (The capsules must be taken at the very beginning of a meal; if taken afterwards they may 'repeat', or cause indigestion. They can be obtained from any chemist). Vegetarians should seek medical advice about taking one or two tablets of vitamin B_{12} daily, to avoid the risk of developing pernicious anaemia, for a preliminary blood test is essential to prevent possible confusion later.

Few elderly people drink enough fluid, yet it is important to do so. Not only must the bladder be flushed out frequently, to prevent its becoming infected and so a troublesome discomfort, but also there are waste products which are better out of the body than in it, and the way to get rid of them is by the urine.

In general, every person should have at least three pints of fluid a day. This is about three times as much as most elderly people in fact have. Those who have been taking too little should gradually increase their fluid intake each day. Curiously enough, people who drink plenty are usually less troubled with urinary discomfort than those who drink little: this is partly because the urine in the latter is concentrated, strong and irritating, and partly because of the infection of the bladder which frequently is due to stagnation of small quantities of urine within it. But care should be taken not to have large quantities of fluid within three or four hours of going to bed. In certain diseases there may be medical restriction of fluid, as there may be of salt (which all elderly people should anyhow take in strict moderation): but, for most, plenty of fluid is important in maintaining health and a feeling of well-being.

Our internal organs will continue to serve well if they are treated reasonably. Like the rest of the body, they lose their elasticity and ability to respond to sudden changes or to excess. Let all changes be gradual: once they have been effected, adhere to them, for it is our nature to follow a well-worn groove when we become old. It is important that it should be a good groove, sensibly adapted to our likes and dislikes and allowing for them.

Chapter 19

THE PHASE OF TRANSITION

I T is something to be born, as the saying is, with a silver spoon in your mouth. It probably means a great deal more to be born into a good home, whether it be rich or poor. But of all our inherited endowments, the most important are the small endocrine glands, some paired, some single, which control and regulate our mental, physical and sexual progress, as well as the day to day working of our bodies. The principal gland, the pituitary, is hidden away at the base of the brain, inside the skull, and is not much larger than a hazel nut. The two adrenal glands lie inside the abdomen above each kidney. The thyroid gland, in the neck, is better known to the average reader, as will be the sex glands external in the male but hidden inside the abdomen in the female. These and others are engaged on their highly specialized functions all our days.

But they are not static. From before birth they individually increase their functioning so that the body may develop and mature to reach a peak of mental and physical activity in most people between 20 and 30: thereafter each gland diminishes or tends to diminish its activities.

The 'teens' are a difficult phase for many: think of the difference between an individual at 13 and so soon afterwards at 20. There is a relatively sudden change from childhood to the responsibilities of being an adult, very often in the teeth of an older generation which finds it hard to accept that 'children' have become self-sufficient and self-supporting with minds of their own.

Very roughly, it is convenient to look at 12-20 years as the phase of development, at 20-35 of adulthood, at 35-50 of maturity, and at 50-65 of transition to the lessening needs of the old age which is to follow. Because of the diminishing function of certain of these glands bodily changes begin to be noticed in the late forties and early fifties. It is a perfectly natural and normal progress of events: it is foolish to ignore and wise to accept it, and having knowledge to keep a weather-eye lifting to check any imbalance whilst the body is adjusting itself.

The diabetes of the elderly, for example, usually is not due so much to disease of the pancreas (as it is in younger people) as to too great a lessening of its activity, often in the face of an increasing ability to afford any food which may be desired: so that dieting adjusted to its powers may be all that is required. Diminished activity of the thyroid may cause an increase in weight, though more often the latter is due to eating too much and exercising too little. The adrenal glands function less efficiently, so there is a poorer response to strain with consequent diminution in the elasticity of mind and body which is so great a feature of the phase of adulthood; this would make the body of a woman unfit to stand the stresses of pregnancy and child-bearing and nature prevents it by removing the power to reproduce: since the monthly periodic disturbances in women are then no longer necessary they stop, the Change of life is noticed, and to the many who accept the situation a new and very happy phase of life opens out.

From before birth boys and girls have separate characteristics and long before puberty have differing aptitudes and interests, due to the action of some of these glands: but at puberty in both the sex glands mature and the power to reproduce becomes developed, taking some years to attain its maximum. In women fertility wanes before it comes to its end at the Change, which occurs almost without exception before 55 years of age: in men it persists as a rule for much longer and may do so in some individuals up to 80 years or more, though in them it has been lessening for twenty or thirty years without disappearing altogether.

The sexual inclinations which become active at puberty in both sexes simultaneously with the appearance of the power to reproduce, may and often do persist in some women for decades after the menopause to an advanced age as in some men. If they fail to do so, it is often not so much due to an insufficiency in the 'sex' and similar glands (even though reproduction is no longer possible) as to a lack of interest by one or other partner. In men as in women the mind and emotions have a profound influence on sexual activity. Many married couples, who have worked out over the years a satisfying relationship, are able in the sixties and seventies to continue an intimate association which, though inevitably modified by diminishing physical powers, is comforting and gives much happiness. Should it persist—but in how many, many marriages it never happens at any time—there is nothing wrong or harmful in it; what was primarily a physical relationship has become the basis of a spiritual union, of tender affection and friendship.

Nervous and emotional disturbances affect some middle-aged women; but they also occur in some men. How much such upsets are a side effect of glandular disturbance and how much is due both in men and women to new limitations which may unconsciously be resented, it is difficult to say. In a woman the cessation of the monthly periods, however welcome this may be in itself and although to many it is the gateway to a fuller and more active existence, is a much more definite indication that she has entered a new phase of life than any similar signal a man has to pass. Both sexes very naturally and properly dislike the progressive physical changes, of having to play a less active part in the world and give way to the succeeding generations. Men in the fifties and sixties may react against the apparent lessening of their sexual power—it is in fact usually their diminished ability to attract: where the decline in sexual power or attraction is markedly greater than that of the sexual impulse, there is an increased liability at this age for offences against society or the law to occur. Patience, and a sympathetic understanding of the unconscious unsettlement and distress of mind which cause the symptoms, with a little firmness and applied commonsense, can do much to tide the sufferer over this difficult phase.

In the past, the severe mental depression or agitation which afflicted some women in later life was looked upon as being due to the Change; the possibility caused, and still causes, much fear and apprehension, not least because the illness of mind may happen to anyone. In fact it does not occur with any great frequency: but like paralytic strokes or poliomyelitis, those which do happen stick in our memory. The truth is, first, that when it occurs it usually does so some years after the monthly periods have completely ceased and the Change is regarded as a thing of the past; second that it happens also to men. Look at Nebuchadnezzar. If you will read the first four chapters of the book of Daniel, you will see how his illness of mind grew, how Daniel gained his confidence by a remarkable bluff, and how the king later became insane. Women are not the only sufferers, but it happens more often to them.

This is a complication of the phase of transition. Why it occurs we do not as yet understand, but something similar happens occasionally to women after childbirth. As people become older, and at childbirth, they are less well able to stand up to strains and stresses, and this kind of mental illness is usually ascribed to worries of all sorts. But which of us is free from some sort of worry? It would seem that for some reason the back has become unfitted to the burden. The secret probably lies in a loss of balance of the endocrine glands, maybe in the production of only one of the many substances they manufacture.

The really important thing is, however, that within the last decade new methods have made the proper treatment and cure of this condition one of the most satisfactory in medicine. Nebuchadnezzar, knowing he was mentally ill, submitted to the primitive 'shock' therapy which Daniel prescribed for him. They drove the king of Babylon, then the greatest nation in the known world, out into the cold and damp of the fields, 'so that his hairs grew like eagles' feathers, and his nails like birds' claws'. Modern methods are kinder, for few constitutions would stand up to this sort of treatment: but note that he got quite well again, and re-assumed his kingship.

It is difficult to understand why so few appreciate the miracles which happen every day. To cure a fulminating pneumonia or meningitis with penicillin: to relieve a labouring and failing heart with tablets and injections and so to prolong life comfortably for many years: to prevent smallpox and diphtheria and typhoid fever: to keep alive and active and well those with diabetes and pernicious anaemia and other formerly fatal diseases: to be able to cure quickly, and completely, those cases of mental illness which, uncommon though they may be, yet can attack any man or woman, are these not miracles of healing in the best sense of the word?

Chapter 20

A MEDICAL CHAPTER

I HEARTS ARE TRUMPS

B Y the time anyone reaches 70, it is probable that his heart will have beat something like three thousand million times, without stopping for a second of rest in all those years. This is a staggering thought and a reassuring one. People often worry about their hearts, but it is very difficult to estimate the reserves of an old heart, which is liable to go on beating in the most surprising and encouraging way in spite of difficulties. This is because the weaklings are weeded out in or before the fifties, and those who survive into the seventies have hearts of splendid quality which may show signs of wear and tear but which do not seem to know how to stop. People who are past 70 don't need to think any more about their hearts than they do about old and trusted —and tough—friends. If the heart shows signs of being tired in later life, modern medicine can do much to help people who are reasonable, and usually without much invalidism either.

It is usual for the heart to beat more slowly with increasing years. On the other hand, in some people there is not only an increase in the rate but also the rhythm becomes irregular. If it continues to beat like this for long, it becomes less efficient and symptoms will appear, simply because it is not having a proper pause between each beat and so is getting tired unnecessarily. This irregular beating does not as a rule arise from a serious condition so much as from natural changes due to age. It is usually possible to slow the heart rate to a reasonable speed, and to relieve any clogging of the circulation, and so the symptoms will disappear. The treatment of an ageing heart is one of the most satisfying things in all the range of medical care.

Every elderly or old person, whether or not his heart is beginning to show signs of tiredness, should look upon stairs, hills, and high winds—especially cold east and boisterous west winds

—as his enemies. When going for a walk, he ought to start with the wind or the hill against him; otherwise he may venture further than he should, and find great difficulty in getting home without excessive strain. A heart treated fairly and sensibly will do its best for an owner who has conserved its reserves. Those who cannot walk as far as they would like at a normal speed can probably manage the desired distance if they go more slowly, or if they pause more often.

II FEAR NO EVIL

Too many people worry about what their blood pressure is or may be: especially if it is said to be high. The truth is that it is normal for the pressure to become raised as we grow older. By the natural processes of ageing, arteries tend to harden: this must mean that for blood to be pumped to the organs and muscles in sufficient quantities the heart has to work harder to raise the pressure to the level necessary to force it through the narrowed tubes. It is because these changes begin to occur in the late twenties and early thirties that from then on all become less and less well able to run far and fast, to give only one example. The first signs of increasing years appear as early as this in most.

It is a fact that if a man does not know that his blood pressure is raised he is much less likely to suffer from symptoms than if he does. So often it is a matter of ill-digested learning. If he does not—as he cannot—really appreciate the position should he learn that there is something not quite usual with his heart, or his blood pressure, or his arteries, naturally and reasonably he worries far more than the situation warrants. Not a few turn themselves into semi-invalids on the strength of some chance words, perhaps spoken without thought by the doctor and misheard or misunderstood by the patient. In the seventies it is quite a good thing to have a pressure reasonably raised: it is not unnatural, and it need not cause alarm. It is wisest to leave a doctor to sort things out for the best and to be guided by his advice. Most old people would be better with a raised blood-pressure than a low one, for they could then expect to be likely to lead a full and active life with a pressure increased to meet the normal changes of the years. There are exceptions to every rule: there are some people whose arteries do not harden and thicken with age, and whose blood pressure in consequence does not need to rise.

What is at the back of the minds of most people whose blood pressure is said to be raised is the fear of a stroke. There is in fact a greater danger of its over-tiring a heart which has to work harder to maintain the increased pressure, but the heart adapts itself in the most remarkable way if changes come slowly and it is treated fairly. If a rule of moderation is observed it will keep jogging along steadily as it has been doing for so many years. None the less, the thought of a stroke, and of lying paralysed and bedridden for months or years, is one which reasonably is in the minds of many elderly folk. Now there are two kinds of stroke.

In one, there is a weakness in the wall of a blood-vessel in the brain. One day the weak place may give way, and there will then be a haemorrhage. This may happen at any age, but it is obviously more likely to occur to people with a very high blood pressure than to those in whom it is merely raised, normal, or low. What really matters is the presence of a weak spot in the wall of a blood-vessel of the presence of which no one can be aware. It is dramatic, but not so very common, and most people whom one thinks may have such an illness go on and on quite happily.

The second kind of stroke is that caused by a clot forming in a blood vessel in the brain. This occurs more commonly than is realized, not only in the brain but also in other organs of the body. It may happen to anyone, even those in the forties and fifties, no matter what the blood pressure is, and to the very old it may come as a gentle friend. Those in whom it causes damage to the nervous system sufficiently severe to cause prolonged confinement to bed, or other serious troubles, are relatively few. With modern methods of treatment a considerable proportion of patients who would formerly have been condemned to uselessness and bed are now given such care after the attack that when recovery in the nervous system begins to take place the paralysed muscles will be ready again to function.

Most, however, only have a passing condition, or so-called 'little' stroke. There may be some weakness of one hand, or an arm, or a leg, or even one side of the body, or a temporary attack of confusion or giddiness, which clears up largely or completely in a week or two and sometimes in a few hours. It is recorded of the great French scientist Louis Pasteur that he had no less than fifty-eight attacks, but continued his incomparable work. These are not so much things of which to be afraid as reminders that we are mortal. Life holds many uncertainties, and chance governs us all our days. In this, as in much else, we must accept what we cannot foresee or prevent. Fortunately, by the time they are old, most have learned to place their faith in a Good Providence, and very few worry about what may happen tomorrow.

III COMMON SENSE ON CANCER

Cancer causes one death in six. This chapter designs to try to help you not to be that sixth one. From time to time all of us think, 'This can't be happening to me', when it is. Cancer can happen at any age: but should it do so to you there is a very good chance that it will not kill you if your eyes are open ordinarily wide. There is no need to go looking for trouble; there is no sense in ignoring it if it is there to see.

It is a short-sighted policy to run away from what is unpleasant. No matter how curable a cancer may be it will involve treatment or an operation; but operations and anaesthetics these days have few terrors. There are certain kinds of cancer which are curable only with difficulty, and given good fortune. What I wish to do is to bring to your notice those which are readily curable if they are taken in reasonable time. For your safety, that can never be too soon.

Never too soon because the cancer which has not spread beyond the organ in which it originates practically never kills. Fingers of growth creep or are carried from it, along tiny channels to glands which are dotted her and there about the body.

Once the growth has reached these glands, it is more difficult to eradicate even with our modern methods of treatment, but not impossible. Only if from any one of these glands it spreads all over the body is it medically incurable: even then much can be done to relieve.

The great difficulty with practically all cancers is that in the stage when they can most readily be dealt with they cause no pain, the general bodily health is good, there has quite possibly been no loss in weight, and the symptoms appear so quietly. It may seem much more sensible to go on a long-planned holiday than to have an operation, or to defer investigation until after your return, or to put off seeking advice for one reason or another. Yet you will be wrong to do so, especially if your symptoms have much in common with what I write below, or something happens which may make you think that you need advice. In some hospitals certain kinds of cancer are looked upon as emergencies, and admitted within a few days of first being seen. This is because it is so essential to deal with them before the crucially important spread from the primary site has taken place. You may feel that you have not the time, that your family affairs need you. Make the most of your life here and take care that your family or business may not, too early, be deprived of the help you best can give them. Never delay seeking advice if it seems desirable, or having investigations done if you are advised to have them.

In women, some very common kinds are not only among the most easily cured of all cancers, but are not usually difficult to diagnose. In spite of the modern more general appreciation of what may be involved, a lump in the breast, especially if it be a small one, or a discharge from the nipple, is still too often noticed and ignored by a woman for long before she sees her doctor. Many such swellings are not cancerous but only an expert can say for sure. Not many women are now more afraid of the possibility of having a 'deformity' than of dying of a growth: because although it was natural and understandable even if unwise, there is now wide knowledge that modern surgeons are artists with great resources, and it is always their aim to leave as small a scar as possible compatible with a good result. It would probably be fair to say that a cancer of the breast, dealt with when the lump is really first noticed, can usually be cured.

Unusual haemorrhage from the front passage in women always calls for advice, especially if it occurs after the cessation of the monthly periods. In the earlier stages of life the majority are harmless enough but it is always wise to seek guidance if only because they will cause anaemia and debility. Most women, almost all who have borne children, have a little harmless white discharge; but if this should change colour, or become watery and more especially if it be streaked with blood or if there are occasional perhaps very slight haemorrhagic losses, advice should be sought.

Cancers of the skin are much more common in the old of both sexes than in the middle-aged, and they are usually so readily and painlessly curable that there is every reason for seeking guidance. Any ulcer of the skin or lip or tongue which does not heal, or a warty eruption which is becoming larger, or any blemish (especially if of long-standing) which begins to increase in size or to change in character, should be suspect. Age or infirmity is rarely a bar to treatment, because it is usually so simple.

Three other sites call for special mention. Advice should be sought if indigestion develops, not so much the flatulent windy type which is fairly common in those who enjoy their food too well, but discomfort or pain coming on soon after food and rather persistent with a tendency to loss of weight because of the disturbance of appetite. It is a difficult subject, because indigestion is common enough, and may have many causes, but this isn't quite like the usual indigestion, and anything unusual calls for guidance.

Next, if there is a change in the bowel habit without obvious reason, especially if there is alternating constipation followed by loose motions: if there is slime with the motions, or a watery discharge, perhaps rather offensive or irritating, from the back passage: or if the motions are streaked with blood; these may be warning signals, and advice should be sought. Haemorrhoids, more popularly called piles, cause the loss of streaks or small quantities of bright blood, and are nothing to worry about, but even so any loss of blood is better checked than neglected, and advice from your doctor is desirable.

Thirdly, there is the passage of blood in the urine. This is easy to notice, and so wise to have treated when you first notice it. The proportion of good results can be most satisfactory, whatever the cause. Neglect it, and the least you can expect is a progressing anaemia.

I have left unmentioned a great variety of other conditions because it seems best to be simple. I don't want you to go seeing cancer everywhere. But the middle-aged and elderly should have any sign of wear and tear corrected so that old age may as far as possible be free from troubles we will then ill be able to meet. As we grow older cancer seems to become less and less vindictive and to grow and spread more slowly, but it still remains.

There is no doubt that the day will soon be with us when surgery for cancer will be a thing of the past. But that day has not yet dawned, and even when it does early diagnosis will still be needed. It will herald another great increase in the number of those who will become old because of the conquests of science. These conquests have already been far-reaching; they are at your disposal if you will be guided to seek advice on anything which is unusual and especially on the particular points I have stressed.

This book may be read by many, but it is intended for you— you *personally*—you who, where ever you are, sit reading what I am writing this quiet summer Sunday morning before breakfast with the bell for early service ringing from the church across my orchard. Somewhere, some day, because of these words, someone may find courage to face his fears. If that were the one thing this book were ever to do, the time, the trouble, the study, the anxiety of mind that each chapter should be clear and helpful, all these would be so very well worth while because someone will have been preserved from so great an evil.

If you consult your doctor, be fair to him. Describe your symptoms clearly and fully, and don't hide anything. If he cannot find much wrong but they persist or get worse, wait for a few weeks, a month or so, and then see him again. Judgment is not easy. He is the only person who can help you if need be, or reassure you if your fears are groundless.

IV THE FALL OF THE LEAVES

Each year, from about the middle of November to the end of January, I see a number of patients, some elderly but most of them old, who tell me that they feel listless and disinclined for the things they normally do. Perhaps it starts with a cold but quite often it just seems to happen. When I have assured myself that they are having enough of the right kind of food and that they have no serious disease, I repeat the promise that I make each year—that if they will be patient until the sap in the trees starts rising and the leaves return, they will be well again: and that they will feel better and stronger and will do more work and better work in the spring and summer if they do not force themselves in the winter to do things for which they feel this unusual disinclination.

This advice I have given for many years, and for many years I have watched patients who have followed it blossom out again in the spring. Indeed, once they have grasped the fact and accepted it, they seem to do much better the next winter. In youth and manhood the cold months are to many the time of greatest activity, stimulating and quickening; but with advancing years first extreme cold, then just ordinary winter weather, slows people and makes them seek warmth and shelter.

'Old folk are at their best in the summer and early autumn.' That was the observation of the Roman physician Celsus two thousand years ago: it is still true today. It seems sensible to think that with the colder weather the circulation grows more sluggish, and probably the blood pressure falls a little. With the coming of spring, these return to their 'normal'. If older people will accept the guidance of their bodies and, without being lazy, let things slide a little, and as much as possible 'sit by the fire and sew', they will be wise. But if they try to go against their physical feelings, and force themselves to do things they have always been accustomed to doing, they will not benefit so much from the changing seasons. Sooner or later it happens to everyone—sometimes before they reach 75, sometimes after—and it is nothing in the least to be alarmed about. It is nature having its way, encouraging the elderly to conserve their energies during the dark days—that they may better enjoy the sunny hours.

What they should do is to economize in effort so that they have more rest, perhaps go out less in bad weather, and cut down the heavy work. They should keep hands and heads busy even if they use their bodies less and find they are taking an unaccustomed nap in the afternoon. They should continue in work if it is suitable, but start a little later, finish a little earlier, and stay at home on bad days. Each year those who notice this feeling must see the doctor to be sure their general health is good: this is very important indeed.

There is one kind of weather which especially affects the aged, and that is when there is snow about. It upsets and depresses them even if they are in a warm room indoors. There is little one can do about it, and it is in itself nothing of which to be afraid. If they will keep quiet and warm they will have done their best to ensure that when it passes they will return to their former well-being. The only ones who suffer real harm from snow are those who ignore it and carry on as usual, for in the later years people are very sensitive to the elements of nature, and some pay dearly for an experience which is of no value to them. In childhood, with life to face, it is not good to be too fearful of danger: when we are old it is wisdom to avoid it.

So be careful to keep up your standards, to keep warm, and to have enough good food, for it is very easy, and very wrong, to fail to do so when feeling low because the leaves are off the trees, and the barometer is low.

Chapter 21

PREVENTION OF ACCIDENTS

A danger foreseen is half-avoided
English Proverb c. 1730

T H E old are more liable to serious accidents than any other age group. Not only do these cause shock to the system always, and pain and suffering usually; but their effects may linger, to limit activity and affect health. Rheumatism, and the effects of a previous accident, have been found to be the two commonest conditions leading to prolonged ill-health and disability in the later years.

Accidents do not just happen: they are always caused, and are usually due to carelessness by somebody. What few appreciate are the simple reasons why they are so liable to happen to the old, and so can avoid or prevent them. With a better understanding but without being too fussy, much might be saved.

Many men and women only realize for the first time that they are growing old when they find themselves subject to disturbances of balance. They will already have remarked that any movements they make are performed more slowly than in the past, but this is something which begins to happen in the twenties. You never come downstairs as fast as when you are a schoolboy, three or four at a time and six at the bottom; and whilst they may not have occasion to do this in the thirties, few could if they tried.

Usually in the seventies, even if health is otherwise good, most people find that co-operation between head and legs is waning. It is not just a matter of going sedately as it has been up to then. The new changes are an extension of earlier ones, but they are more noticeable and from the practical point of view more likely to bring harm. So it is well to be aware in advance, and when they occur not to be unduly alarmed, for what to do will be known.

There is a sense within the joints which tells the brain about the position and movements of the limbs, and this is impaired to a greater or lesser extent in the elderly and old. It is largely because of this loss that a sliding rug, a slippery floor, a small patch of ice, an unexpected step up or down or a gentle slope, or trying to move about in a jolting bus, may have them all at sea unless they are careful to have a hold with at least one hand. These most commonly cause falls when people are doing things as a matter of course because they have always done them. When standing on two feet on a stable surface they are secure: but if they put all the weight on one leg for a moment, they are liable to overbalance and fall heavily when restoring their position to normal. This is partly because the defective joint sense does not convey sensations to the brain sufficiently quickly, and partly because the muscular reactions have also become sluggish. It is a wise precaution for the elderly to train themselves as far as possible to sit when putting on shoes, tying the laces, cutting toenails, tending the feet in or out of the bath, or when pulling on trousers or pants, and thus avoid any action which will call for putting all the stationary weight even for a moment on one leg. Every year many people fall, and fall heavily, because they put one foot on a chair when attending to it, over-balance when lowering it to the ground, and have no handhold to preserve their balance. For the same reason it is safer to go up or down stairs which have a hand-rail, and there should always be one hand free with which to grasp it or to steady oneself against a wall. Climbing on to a chair for whatever reason is dangerous; it should not be attempted unless at least one hand has a secure hold, and under no circumstances should there be anything heavy in the other. After stooping to a low cupboard or light switch it may be found that the knees seem to fail. If possible shelves should be within easy reach, as should the gas or electricity meter. This deficiency of joint sense is the commonest and least well recognized of all the causes of injury in the later years. It is hard to accustom one-self to it because to have to stop, or to take greatly increased care, goes against the grain when doing things which seem quite natural.

Simple weakness of the muscles makes it difficult for some to lift their feet, so they shuffle about and may catch a toe on quite small things like a rug or an irregularity in the floor. Electric flexes when worn and covered by a rug or carpet cause many fires and burns and the only safe thing to do is to get them altogether out of the way. Muscular weakness and the slow reactions of the elderly are not only the cause of some accidents but the reason why any tumble is liable to be severe. They are unable to save themselves from falling like a sack of coals, or fail to recover themselves when they do fall and quickly move away from anything (like a fire) which may inflict further injury.

All elderly people need a good light especially on stairs and at dark corners. Care should be taken not to leave things about on the floor or stairs, for if the light is bad or sight is poor they may be forgotten and cause a trip or stumble; then any lessening of the sense of balance will cause a fall. Darkness is a very real difficulty to old people who not only may get completely lost in their own bedrooms, but find themselves to be less steady on their feet in the dark. The risk of an injury is obvious and if an electric bed light is not possible, a night light is a sensible cheap precaution if used with proper care: many have to get out in the night, or wish to get themselves a cup of tea from a bedside thermos or to go downstairs to make one.

II

After 75 any tendency to giddiness rapidly increases. As many as three out of every four women aged over 85 suffer from it, and the rate of accidents rises closely parallel. Deafness is often associated with giddiness, for the balancing mechanism is as liable to wear out as that of hearing. So much happiness and comfort is governed by the little things; this is one of the smallest yet most disturbing, and since it cannot be opposed it is fortunate that with care much can be avoided.

You may find one day that if you look up or turn the head suddenly, there will be giddiness for a moment or two; all that can be done is to rest in a convenient position until it passes off.

It is important that control should be learned as early as possible. Those who have severe attacks do in fact sometimes fall down, but this is not usual. To struggle along, taking no precautions, will lead to loss of confidence, which may progress to a severe degree of inactivity; and sufferers may be afraid to walk about unaided and so sit for hours in a chair only moving when there is a helping hand nearby. When that happens it is not usually very long before they are kept 'safely' in bed.

Tight collars should not be worn. Deliberation of movement must be learned, as must performing slowly and carefully the actions which are known to induce an attack; such as turning the head or the eyes or the body quickly, looking upwards, bending or stooping, or getting quickly up out of bed, or off a couch, or a chair after a meal.

There need be no alarm felt at this giddiness by those who are careful. It is a natural if unpleasant symptom and one must learn to take care and to guard against its consequences. It is important that invalidism should not be established simply because the fear of falling is a cause of alarm to others. The remedy largely rests with the individual for in general medical care can achieve relatively little though a proportion can be helped. If sleeping or sedative tablets are being taken, medical advice *must* be sought for some of these drugs are liable to aggravate any tendency to giddiness and falls, especially at night.

III

Other common injuries are burns and scalds: many of these are associated with falls. But each year some old people are severely or fatally burned because they smoke in bed or read in bed with a candle, drop off to sleep, and the bedclothes catch fire. Human nature being what it is, old people usually pay little attention to warnings. So it is wise when elderly not to start anything which may be harmful when old. By spending a pound or two one can have a proper electric bedside light fitted instead of a candle in case it is desired to read at bedtime or during the night, as many do. Should one use a fireguard? If there has been a tumble for a trivial reason, if you are liable to fall asleep in a chair, or if you are subject to attacks of giddiness, you certainly should, and for anyone over 70 it is a wise precaution. This applies to all fires, whether gas, electric, coal or oil.

IV

Accidents in the bathroom are common. Fear puts many elderly people off having a daily bath: this is a pity, for all are better for one. A chair in the bathroom allows drying (especially of the feet) and nail-cutting to be done safely and in comfort, and obviates the need at any time to stand on one leg without a hand grip. A rubber mat on the floor of the bath may slip, but is often very helpful. A hand grip on the bath or the wall is better than nothing, but the most satisfactory arrangement is a safety rail which is attached to the taps. With a rubber mat in the bath, this provides maximum safety at a very reasonable cost. The same firm*also makes a seat to fit inside the top of the bath which allows adequate bathing without full immersion.

V

At present there is only limited knowledge of the effects of long continued living on a diet deficient in some of what are believed to be essentials. Many people have definite opinions but relatively few have facts to back them. There are good grounds for believing that a diet defective in quality (whatever its merits as regards quantity) tends to be one, and possibly the most important, of the causes of the muscular weakness of the old. There is no doubt that a defective diet affects the nutrition of the bones so that they become brittle and break more easily, and in my experience this particular accident most often affects those who do not drink milk. After an accident, especially one causing the breaking of a limb, any former deficiencies in the diet will retard recovery.

It is in the interest of everybody, but most of all of ourselves, that preventable accidents should be prevented. It is foolish to

* C. Winn and Co., Granville Street, Birmingham 1.

146

expect to be without some of the infirmities which come with increasing years. It is folly to deny them, to try to bluff ourselves about giddiness or eyesight, hearing, or the weakness of our limbs. Honest acceptance is not only better, but is appreciated by others. If we become subject to one or other of the failings of age there is no occasion to become depressed about it. They are tedious, tiresome, and add to the difficulties in the face of diminishing pleasures and interests. But at least most of them are not painful: unless we ignore them and then the consequences may cause us much discomfort.

Chapter 22

THE FAITH OF SOME OLD FRIENDS

WHETHER or not you accept the accuracy of my observations on this difficult because delicate subject is not important if I stimulate you to think, and then look into your own heart and to see what you find there. But I have reason to believe that what I write represents the opinions of many ordinary people.

The old believe in God. Not the fatherly God we were taught about as children—many of us are parents and grandparents ourselves, and know only too well the failings of fathers which the children do not realize. Nor is He the active Deity whose unceasing purpose may background our minds in the years of maturity and middle-age. Gradually we come to accept a God whom we do not in the least understand, but in whom we have trust. Seventy years and more teach us that we have had so much for which to be thankful, that there are others worse off than we, that life has always been uncertain and now is increasingly so, but that faith in Divine Providence is faith well placed. This comes to us not out of books, and not out of preaching and sermons, but from within ourselves. Experience has taught us how much goodness and kindness there is in the world, often coming to us from unexpected sources. Experience has taught us that troubles pass, that if we persevere problems and difficulties will be overcome in one way or another, that the aches and pains of everyday life and its disabilities can after a time become less noticeable even if hard to bear. And God *is* kind, for He often gently takes away the understanding of the aged, and He does give us some power over the will to live. When we are old most feel we are very close to Him and are not afraid; we commit ourselves into His care and keeping and have no dread of an unknown future for we feel in close communion with Him.

To the old, the human Jesus is in general a vague and indefinite figure. He is a young man, in the eyes of most, and we

148

are old. In childhood and manhood it is not too difficult in some way to identify ourselves with Him: and, maybe, if we can a little forget His Divinity, find help and comfort in the realization that through personal experience He would understand our difficulties. But He never experienced old age. He taught and showed a way of life for men to follow, but it was a brief life which ended in His early death at 33: and we are past 70, maybe past 80. We may follow the pattern of worship which has guided us all our years from childhood on, but not many have the faith consciously to accept His influence on their lives now, whatever it may once have been. But some of us remember that after His Resurrection He returned to His Father, and is God, and so we do not think of Him as a man at all.

There are exceptions and some cannot tolerate the thought, but in old age few have any dread of the end. We do not think about it over-much, any more than we think much about the possibility of some illness laying us low. We live from day to day without looking very far into the unknown future partly because experience has taught us the wisdom of so doing, and partly because life is still so full of changes—even in our wearing bodies—that it is interesting. This is not to say that when we do think about it we like the prospect of leaving the world; most of us want to go on living, even if we suffer. But we do not regret with the intensity of those younger than we, who have to face it with the knowledge that they will be denied decades of living, that their best and most useful and fruitful years could have lain ahead, or that they have prematurely to leave behind those for whom their love promised happiness and the joy of service. Old people who have had a hard life tend to keep their mental faculties better than those who have had an easy one, for they have solved their own problems and have not run away from them: so they do not run away from this prospect either. Devotion to Divine Providence is a very natural thing in old age however shallow our 'religious' beliefs may seem to us. There are hardships of which only God and we are aware, and which our nearest and dearest (if we are so fortunate as to have any who care) cannot appreciate, and so we come to share them with Him. How then, can we fear to return whence we came? We know that when we are called we must go.

Indeed, not a few, though we may shrink from an unknown future, are curious: we very much want to know what is going to happen after the long-familiar 'now'. Some of us have a complete and absolute faith in an after-life because St John xiv vv. 2 and 3 states it clearly and the promise therein is sure. But for most our view is clouded: what happened to our parents and grandparents will now soon be happening to us, and in time will happen to our children, our neighbours and friends, those whom we like and dislike, all the people in the world; we have a feeling that there may, or may not, be an after-life, but whichever we incline to we don't know, and nobody else does, it is all hidden behind the mist, beyond our imagination and for many beyond their beliefs.

Few of us pray much when we are old though I know that some pray more, and pray more earnestly and consistently than in their younger days. Most forget that they still have a part they can play in the world, even if it is silent, hidden and un-noticeable. Indeed, among the wisest and happiest old people are those who every few hours pause for a while—they have the time—and sit quietly in a chair to speak to God and to let Him speak to them. It is true that opportunities for supporting our thoughts with sacrifices and acts of kindness are now very limited, but if they occur we will be happier if we take them; and unless we are quite cut off from the world they do happen.

Chapter 23

A SIMPLE RULE OF LIFE

I

S I T down each day to a cooked midday meal. Have a pint of new milk every day; at least half of it should be taken fresh, warm or in a warm (not boiled) drink, and the rest, if desired, can be made into pudding or junket and so on; the top of the milk makes stewed fruit and many other things much more appetizing. Have brown bread rather than white. Have some fresh red meat, or fish, or an egg, once every day, and liver once a fortnight; these are expensive but you will not need much, and they are of the highest importance. Lastly, have green vegetables and fresh fruit; a raw apple or an orange or their equivalent every day will suffice.

You need have only a light breakfast; perhaps a cereal with fresh milk and sugar, or an egg and tea with toast or brown bread and marmalade to follow. There is no better or cheaper supper, and it is easily prepared, than porridge—using quick cooking oats with fresh milk and black treacle (treacle is not only nourishing but an excellent mild laxative such as most need): alternatively bread and cheese and a glass of milk or bread and milk sprinkled with sugar.

It is undesirable that food should be dull, but for those who are poor most of the variety must be in the midday meal. To those with more money a much wider choice is available but the above are the minimal essentials if health is to be maintained.

II

Be sure to keep warm, for in later life fuel can be as important as food. It is not only a matter of having a warm room in which to sit. The bed should be warm, and the nightclothes, and the chill off the bedroom before it is entered. Especially in winter it is wise to have a bed-sitting-room, because it can always be warm without undue expense. To sit in a cold room is a great mistake, even if you persuade yourself you prefer it that way, and 'fresh' air can do more harm than good, especially to 'chesty' people, though stuffiness is to be avoided. It is a simple medical fact that cold reduces the vitality, depresses activity and the pursuit of interests, and predisposes to ill-health, more than any other single factor save lack of proper food: and this especially applies to the old in whom the mechanism for regulating the internal temperatures of the body is not so efficient as in the young.

III

Have help in the home when it is needed.

IV

Try not to let your life get narrow.

Chapter 24

FROSTY BUT KINDLY

Therefore my age is as a lusty winter
Frosty but Kindly
        As You Like It, Act 2, Scene 2

'I DON'T feel conscious of approaching 80 any more that I felt conscious of reaching 60 or 70, or any more than I shall feel conscious of reaching 90', Sir Thomas Beecham said on the day before his eightieth birthday.

Life can be as pleasant during the later years of retirement as in the earlier, or any other age. Even when there are disabilities, most find much happiness because they have learned to accept things over which they have no control. People should look forward to these later years with quiet confidence because once there they really are on the Other Side of the Hill: and the road, it will be found, will be adapted to failing legs.

In the writing of this book I have been able to draw on my association with those who saw me come to my villages about thirty years ago as the Young Doctor. Some have passed on, some who were then around 50 have grown old as I have matured and gathered experience. My old friends and I have come to know each other and trust each other—the enduring foundation of the second half of one's lifetime in general practice.

I have more than sixty patients aged over 75: but few of them are old in heart or aged in mind, and their bodies mostly retain a surprising vitality. Even if it may present difficulties in management and attention is needed more frequently, the care of the old-in-years from the purely medical point of view is usually easier than that of the younger generations. So many things are worn yet seem to keep on working passably well. All the organs have been tested and tried out for so long that we know from experience that they are of Rolls-Royce quality, and will go on and on if they are treated reasonably and not tinkered with too much. The signs are of wear rather than of wearing out.

We all have to learn to accept the simple fact that people do not grow younger, but only older. Some age quickly, notably those who are most pre-occupied with their health and themselves: most do so slowly, because they are absorbed in living. Some never seem to age at all: they are the few with warm hearts and lively minds, who are young no matter what their score in years, the evergreens. Age in years is so infinitely less important than age of mind.

Many people facing the later years are filled with fear of possible oncoming frailties, and the greater fear of becoming unnecessary or unloved. It is helpful to remember that when inquiry was made of 21,000 old people in Salford, an industrial town, only 1,500 required any type of service. Trust in the Good Providence which has guarded and guided for so many years and preserved from so many evils is indeed well-placed.

To people at most ages their years hardly seem to belong to them at all. As we become middle-aged, then elderly, later old, we have to recall the changing facts to ourselves again and again consciously: and have continuously to readjust the self-portrait which each of us carries in his mind and to remind ourselves that our position in relation to the rest of the world is continually altering.

One moment we are perhaps getting married and finding it difficult to realize that this is in fact happening to us. Next, almost in a flash, we find ourselves with increasing responsibilities to our families . . . little did we think so few years back that we might so soon have children of our own . . . as well as to those around us. Soon maybe we find that we have progressed a further step, that our children have grown up and left home and that their generation has moved into the centre of the stage. Then we discover that we have retired, become senior citizens.

Yet most of us feel no great change, and it is only by recalling to ourselves that we are middle-aged, elderly, old, that we can keep fitting ourselves into our proper place in our own eyes as well as in those of our world. Nay, we may not realize that in fact we are old until we find that our knees do not obey the instructions of our head or will not readily kneel, or we notice that the hand lying in our lap is the hand of age.

The ebb and flow of strength which accompanies old age, which makes us feel very old one day and surprisingly younger . . . though not young . . . the next, has to be learned and accepted and allowed for. In fact when we were younger we had our better days and our worse days too, but then so great were our reserves that we were able largely to ignore the change or at worst not let it disturb us. When we are old, even in one day the variations in vigour are quite remarkable, and it is difficult for those of another generation to appreciate and so to allow for them.

Mere age alone, devoid of wisdom and virtue, has no lawful claim to reverence. He who can cultivate a calm and contented disposition will hardly feel the pressure of the years and will find a full measure of all the good things which the years ahead can hold for him.

LOOKING BACKWARDS—AND FORWARDS—AT 94

by

J. W. Robertson Scott C.H., M.A. (Hon.) Oxon.

T H E Author suggests that I might select a few paragraphs from a broadcast 'Myself when Old', which the BBC asked me to make from my home at Idbury Manor on my ninety-first birthday. The address was reproduced in *The Listener*, to which I am indebted for my extracts. What I said brought me touching letters from home and overseas. The experience I recited and the sentiments I expressed may be an encouragement to some elderly folk. As a class these people are often kept or keep themselves too much indoors; they do not see many new faces; they often take in an uninspiring newspaper; too commonly they do not see any books that amount to much; they easily get or are getting into the way of thinking that the world is going to the devil, which it isn't. But here are the extracts from a discourse which was headed somewhere *A Cheery Nonagenarian*.

'Do not be sorry for a man in his nineties as I am. He has three advantages. He has seen no end of forebodings of disaster come to nothing. He knows that the many changes that have taken place during his lifetime have been almost wholly for the better. And he has undergone what I call the final discipline. By that I mean that he has usually come through what he may take to be the worst and the best that can happen to him—and to "he" of course I add "she".

'One gift that comes to the ageing is a relish for quiet, an appreciation of being alone. Another gain is a sense of proportion. The aged realize, more and more fully, what is important, what is less important, and what is not important at all. We cease, for instance, to accumulate things. We take time to think. That there are periods in which we are appalled or distressed by

156

what has happened to someone or some people, when our hearts are wrung, is surely to be expected. It is equally to be expected that we should front our trials and rise above them. That is, if we are not merely aged but grown up.

'You may think I am burking recognition of what is the worst to be undergone in the final discipline of old age, continuous loss by death of men and women whose friendship was enjoyment, comfort, stay, and stimulus. You remember Charles Lamb saying that there was no one left to call him "Charley".

'Every morning when I open *The Times* I find myself turning first not to the chief news page but, farther on, to the obituary articles page, in order to see if any man or woman I have known and valued has gone.

'Then, most grievous of all, there is the loss of one's nearest and dearest. One gets lonelier. But every one of us has reserves of courage that can be called up. The strength of these reserves of courage is astonishing.

'Think of the millions of men and women, the world round, at this moment, acquainted with grief. Some people are overcome by grief, in the common phrase are "never the same again". Others refuse to be bowed down, stand up against sorrow; and so get themselves in trim for wrestling with and overcoming the next trial.

'My friend Eden Phillpotts, the novelist, who was ninety-five when I last heard from him, and is still at work, has a character in one of his satisfying stories, who says. "This is more than I can bear". Phillpotts, a loving-hearted man and a rational thinker, adds the words: "This is a sentiment seldom uttered by a man or a woman save under conditions perfectly capable of endurance". Then he quotes the words of Carlyle, "The hero slumbers in every man". Carlyle might have added the heroine in every woman.

'I have frequently passed the spot before Balliol College where Latimer and Ridley were burnt at the stake, and gave us the immortal farewell, "Be of good courage". Think of the thousands and thousands of men and women, of all races of mankind, who, with unconquered minds, have nobly endured. That great spirit, Einstein, left us counsel for all extremities:

"Never despair," he wrote, "go forward. Work unceasingly wherever and whenever you can". That is to say, every single one of us may have the honour of being of the company, however humbly, of the valiant of the earth.

'Think of how our people have advanced. Not more than a century ago the great naturalist parson wrote, "The lower orders are brutalized by horrible suffering, lost in rags and filth, are dying for lack of food".

'It is but a few years since the mass of our people could not read, and if they could have read, had little to read. In our day, education for young and adult alike has become more and more, not a social badge, but a privilege for everyone. Today the phrase, "the poor", in its old use, has gone out of the language. Can we really picture what life was like without telegraphy and telephone (let alone wireless and television), newspapers for everybody, and—for the asking nowadays—competent doctors, efficient dentistry, hearing aids, good spectacles and free library books?

'The other month I chanced to be, between eleven and twelve in the morning, on a hillside above a town of about 3,000 inhabitants. What struck me as I looked was that, at a time when food was being cooked, no smoke was rising from the chimney of any house. Gas or electricity was doing the job. It was one simple illustration of the changes within my lifetime. Think not only of the freedom which what may be called the New Kitchen has given most housewives, but of the fact that in my boyhood not one woman (or, for that matter, not more than a quarter of the population) had a vote. Now, as a matter of course, women are in the Houses of Parliament and in every calling they care to enter.

'The present time can be fairly judged only by informed, unprejudiced, healthy minded men and women who set themselves to think, who are honest enough to recall truly and fully the living conditions, the prevalent beliefs and outlook in their early days, not in one class but in all classes. Of course, today there are plenty of things that are not as we should like them.

'Against all that needs to be bettered there are noteworthy things to be set. Take but one example, free libraries: in my county more than 300 rural libraries, not counting the libraries in the towns of the county. Add to this the prodigious sales of eighteen-penny and half-crown books of a high class. Unquestionably the mind of the nation is being stretched.

'In manpower and in national resources, the human races go on bearing a grievous burden of armaments, by land, sea, and air, at which historians of the future will marvel. But there have been daily signs that the world is slowly but steadily becoming wiser.

'In thinking about the future, our stand-by is a firm grip on the fact that *our civilization is very, very young*. Nonagenarians, on the basis of their experience, have the felicity of watching the development of mankind. Almost the very last has now been heard of the conception of our tiny earth as the centre of the universe, with all that such determined ignorance brought upon us. Instead of "the universe" we have learned to speak of "the universes", billions of them; not millions of miles distant but billions of miles! It is known that an eminent writer of our own day, in his latest years, found in the study of the sky the food his mind needed. In our brief lives, and in all difficulties, there is indeed nothing like pondering the elementary facts of astronomy and history. Pondering them, and also the beauty and wonder of plants and trees, the immense variety of them and of birds, animals, and insects. One has to keep reminding oneself, indeed: hedgehogs, bees, elephants, butterflies, snakes, whales, dogs, birds, giraffes, horses! And the millions of years that went by for the development and growth of every single species! And the millions, it may be billions of years that sentient beings have to go yet!'

Appendix I

HEALTH AND STRENGTH IN OLD AGE

A M O M E N T ' S thought will convince that elderly and aged people who live alone will have more difficulty in solving the physical and financial problems of increasing years than others of their age who have companionship and rarely know loneliness.

In 1954 I was invited by the Oxfordshire Association for the Care of Old People to carry out a survey to pinpoint the needs of old people who lived alone and in 1962 to follow it up with a wider study. These were published in the *Oxford Times*.

It was found that growing old was likely to be more difficult in a town than in a village, but that it is not usually a painful progress. Ninety out of two hundred and fifty-two found no great difficulty, and of these, twenty-five out of seventy-four were aged over 80.

Ninety-six out of two hundred and fifty two, including twenty-three aged over 80, had no special problems. In a study of the biggest physical handicap, one hundred and eight seemed to have none, which included twenty-four aged over 80, discounting mere age.

The principal problem of forty-three individuals was loss of mobility (especially after 75), of twenty-five, impaired health (spread evenly over all age groups), of twenty-seven, loneliness (noticed most before 75), of twenty-five, money problems (also felt most before 75), and of sixteen, physical weakness (especially after 75). Sight and hearing were the principal problems of six (all over 80). The observers found that health (fifty-one) and arthritis (forty-three) were the principal handicaps, followed by physical weakness (twenty), and grossly impaired sight or hearing (sixteen).

It has been observed elsewhere that even at 85 only 65% will be impaired in health and no more than 10% permanent invalids. Given more care by people in their fifties, these figures could be improved and it is open to any individual to look to his own future.

Appendix II

ANNUITIES

A N Annuity is a fixed annual income bought from a Life Assurance Company by the payment of a capital sum. It is known as an Immediate Annuity. The older the purchaser, the higher the income from £100 invested: since women live longer than men, a woman of seventy will pay much the same as a man of sixty-five to obtain an equal benefit.

For example, a man aged sixty-five—or a woman of seventy—who pays down £2,000 can expect an Annuity of about £220 a year paid quarterly or half-yearly in arrears, for the rest of his or her life. This is a far higher income than can be obtained from any reasonably safe investment, but ordinarily at death the capital has disappeared, whether the Annuity has been in force for two weeks or thirty years.

Not all Annuities are of the Immediate kind. By buying instalments, usually during the working life of the annuitant, a Deferred Annuity is often timed to become payable on retirement. This is useful to self-employed persons or employees for whom no special pension provision is made by their employers. It is possible to write into the contract a clause which will ensure the return of premiums to the estate should the annuitant die before the Annuity becomes due, or even to make the Annuity joint on the lives of both husband and wife; although in both these cases the annual payments when due will be smaller, the survivor is protected, which is often more important. In purchasing any Annuity, the more favourable the terms of contract to the annuitant, the more must be paid for specific benefits.

Alternatively, it is possible to purchase an Annuity Certain, which is paid for a specific minimum number of years regardless of whether the Annuitant dies in the meantime: but on this type of Annuity Income Tax may be payable on the whole amount if the annuitant dies and the beneficiary under his will is outside the range of tax reliefs.

Under some Pension Schemes an option exists to commute up to one quarter of the capital value of the pension into cash. This sum can then be invested by an employee in an Annuity for his wife's

L   161

life: but many pension schemes make provision for the wife's protection, if this is sought when the pension becomes due, so there may be no advantage. The best course always is to consult the company's Pension Officer.

Contingent Annuities will fall due for payment only if some specified event occurs. Where a husband's pension ends with his death and would leave his widow without an income, under such a plan she would be protected. The cost is much lower than for an Immediate Annuity because it will be purchased, paid for, and the capital sum invested by the Assurance Company years—sometimes many years—beforehand: moreover there is some chance that the wife will die before her husband, in which case the Annuity will not be payable at all.

Prior to the Finance Act 1956, all income from Annuities was taxed. Since then, the capital content of each annual payment is free of tax, and only the interest element is taxable. The capital content varies with age and is based on the number of years life expectancy of the annuitant, by which the purchase price is divided. For example, a man of sixty-five who paid £2,000 for an Annuity of £220 would receive £140 of this tax free, for his life expectancy is slightly over fourteen years. The interest element is derived from the invested funds of the Assurance Company issuing the Annuity, and this will vary from company to company depending on the investment policy of each. With the current rates of interest, Annuity rates are at a very satisfying level. If there were a return to cheap money, new Annuities would give a lower return than at present. Like Life Insurance premiums, the rate of an Annuity does not diminish once it has been fixed by contract.

Arrangements exist for the Assurance Company to pay Annuities free of tax when the Annuitant's total income is not subject to tax. At the other extreme, a sur-tax payer, or one paying income tax at the full standard rate, should include as income taxed at source only the interest element of Annuity payments—*not* the capital element.

It is up to the purchaser of an Annuity to make the best bargain he can. A return per £100 invested will vary between company and company. A table showing the amounts paid by different Assurance Companies at varying ages will be found in Whitaker's Almanack (standard edition). The following small table shows how the payments made by three large companies vary.

162

Immediate Annuities (payable half-yearly, in arrear) for every
£100 paid

	Males			Females		
	Age 60	Age 65	Age 70	Age 60	Age 65	Age 70
Company A	£9.12.10	£11.1.8	£13.2.6	£8.13.4	£9.14.7	£11.5.0
Company B	£8.14.2	£10.2.10	£12.3.7	£7.13.11	£8.15.10	£10.6.2
Company C	£9.15.6	£11.4.8	£13.6.4	£8.15.8	£9.17.4	£11.8.2

Appendix III

SIMPLE SELF MADE WILLS

I F someone decided to make his own will, took a clean whole un-marked untorn sheet of paper and typed or wrote in ink (not pencil) 'I leave fifty pounds to my son John and a hundred pounds to my daughter Mary and all the rest of my property to my wife whom I appoint to be my executor. This is the last will of John Smith of Honeysuckle Cottage, Somewhere. Dated this seventh day of June nineteen hundred and fifty-eight and signed by the said John Smith in the presence of the undersigned witnesses and by them in his presence and in the presence of each other.' signed it first and got two witnesses to sign it after him, all being present together when this was done, he will have then made a valid will. It is as well to add the addresses and occupations of the witnesses.

A witness, or witness' wife or husband, may not benefit from a will which (s)he has witnessed; the will remains valid but the gift fails. But you MUST sign it in the presence of your witnesses, and they in your presence and that of each other, all being present to-gether. The will should have been written out previously except for *all* the signatures. Since there must NOT be any scratching out or altering the wording or writing in something else without each alteration being initialled by the testator and his witnesses, it is as well first to think out exactly what you are going to do : then make a draft, and finally make a fair copy on a *whole* untorn sheet of paper.

If you wish to alter your will after it has been made, the only things to do are either to make another will, or to add a codicil.

For example John Smith could later take another whole sheet of paper and write, 'I leave ten pounds to my niece Jane Smith. This is a codicil to my will. Dated this tenth day of September nineteen hundred and fifty-eight. Signed by John Smith of Honeysuckle Cot-tage, Somewhere in the presence of the undersigned witnesses and by them in his presence and in the presence of each other'. Then he and two witnesses (not necessarily the same two witnesses as before or either of them) must sign it as for a will.

The codicil should then be kept with the will. The contents of neither will nor codicil have to be disclosed to the witnesses but you should tell them that it is your will or codicil.

Often more wording than the short example above will be necessary, and without legal advice you may make a muddle of it. For example if there is more than one page, each separate page must be signed and witnessed. Much will often depend on its simplicity, even when drawn up by a lawyer.

BIBLIOGRAPHY

AMULREE, LORD: *Adding Life to Years*

ANONYMOUS (Lancet Publications): *Disabilities and How to Live with Them*

CHISHOLM, CECIL: *Retire and Enjoy It*

HARTON, SYBIL: *On Growing Old*

HOPE, MARY: *Towards Evening*

HOWELL, TREVOR: *Our Advancing Years*

LAWTON, G.: *New Goals for Old Age*

NATIONAL COUNCIL OF SOCIAL SERVICE:
Over 70
Living Longer
Age is Opportunity

SCOTT, G., AND WILLIAMS, C. R. S.: *Old People Living Alone, An Oxfordshire Survey (Oxford Times 1954)*

SCOTT, G., ET AL: *Ourselves When Old (Oxford Times 1963)*

SHELDON, J. H.: *The Social Medicine of Old Age*

STAMM, T. T.: *Foot Troubles*

For Product Safety Concerns and Information please contact our EU
representative GPSR@taylorandfrancis.com
Taylor & Francis Verlag GmbH, Kaufingerstraße 24, 80331 München, Germany